Z80 Assembly Language Programming for Students

Macmillan Computer Science Series

Consulting Editor

Professor F. H. Sumner, University of Manchester

S.T. Allworth, *Introduction to Real-Time Software Design*
Ian O. Angell, *A Practical Introduction to Computer Graphics*
R.E. Berry and B.A.E. Meekings, *A Book on C*
G.M. Birtwistle, *Discrete Event Modelling on Simula*
T.B. Boffey, *Graph Theory in Operations Research*
Richard Bornat, *Understanding and Writing Compilers*
J.K. Buckle, *Software Configuration Management*
W.D. Burnham and A.R. Hall, *Prolog Programming and Applications*
J.C. Cluley, *Interfacing to Microprocessors*
Robert Cole, *Computer Communications*
Derek Coleman, *A Structured Programming Approach to Data**
Andrew J.T. Colin, *Fundamentals of Computer Science*
Andrew J.T. Colin, *Programming and Problem-solving in Algol 68**
S.M. Deen, *Fundamentals of Data Base Systems**
S.M. Deen, *Principles and Practice of Database Systems*
P.M. Dew and K.R. James, *Introduction to Numerical Computation in Pascal*
M.R.M. Dunsmuir and G.J. Davies, *Programming the UNIX System*
K.C.E. Gee, *Introduction to Local Area Computer Networks*
J.B. Gosling, *Design of Arithmetic Units for Digital Computers*
Roger Hutty, *Fortran for Computers*
Roger Hutty, *Z80 Assembly Language Programming for Students*
Roland N. Ibbett, *The Architecture of High Performance Computers*
Patrick Jaulent, *The 68000 – Hardware and Software*
J.M. King and J.P. Pardoe, *Program Design Using JSP – A Practical Introduction*
H. Kopetz, *Software Reliability*
E.V. Krishnamurthy, *Introductory Theory of Computer Science*
V.P. Lane, *Security of Computer Based Information Systems*
Graham Lee, *From Hardware to Software – An Introduction to Computers*
A.M. Lister, *Fundamentals of·Operating Systems, third edition**
G.P. McKeown and V.J. Rayward-Smith, *Mathematics for Computing*
Brian Meek, *Fortran, PL/1 and the Algols*
Barry Morrell and Peter Whittle, *CP/M 80 Programmer's Guide*
Derrick Morris, *System Programming Based on the PDP11*
Pim Oets, *MS-DOS and PC-DOS – A Practical Guide*
Christian Queinnec, *LISP*
John Race, *Case Studies in Systems Analysis*
W.P. Salman, O. Tisserand and B. Toulout, *FORTH*
L.E. Scales, *Introduction to Non-linear Optimization*
Peter S. Sell, *Expert Systems – A Practical Introduction*
Colin J. Theaker and Graham R. Brookes, *A Practical Course on Operating Systems*
J.M. Trio, *8086-8088 Architecture and Programming*
M.J. Usher, *Information. Theory for Information Technologists*
B.S. Walker, *Understanding Microprocessors*
Peter J.L. Wallis, *Portable Programming*
I.R. Wilson and A.M. Addyman, *A Practical Introduction to Pascal – with BS6192,
second edition*

*The titles marked with an asterisk were prepared during the Consulting Editorship of Professor J.S. Rohl, University of Western Australia.

Z80 Assembly Language Programming for Students

Roger Hutty

School of Mathematics, Computing and Statistics, Leicester Polytechnic

MACMILLAN

First published 1981
Reprinted 1982, 1983, 1984, 1985, 1986

Published by
MACMILLAN EDUCATION LTD
Houndmills, Basingstoke, Hampshire RG21 2XS
and London
Companies and representatives
throughout the world

Printed in Hong Kong

ISBN 0-333-32295-9

Contents

Preface

This learning text, based on the Z80 Assembly Language, enables a student to develop through suitable exercises and programming practice a professional approach to programming and produce a work of quality. There is an art to programming: it is not enough for a student to know the rules of a language, it is equally important to develop a readable and intelligible program which has style and uses the best techniques.

This book is not an ordinary text book — it is a learning text. It is intended to accompany a course of lectures or be used as the text for a tutor-assisted, self-instructional course. However, it is suitable as a teach-yourself text for students who have an appreciation of computer programming, or who already know a little of the Z80 assembly language. Practising Z80 assembly language programmers may find the text useful for reference purposes.

The text is divided into sixteen chapters. Each chapter can be used as a self-contained unit for teaching purposes to be used for one or two weeks' lectures and tutorial, or as self-instructional unit. Each chapter assumes that a student has satisfactorily completed the previous chapters.

A chapter consists of short narratives; each narrative covers one or two concepts and is followed by an exercise. The narratives move fast, the exercises are challenging and they encourage students to make many discoveries for themselves, thereby allowing the rapid development of skills. Every opportunity is taken to expose practical problems and develop good programming habits right from the start.

The narratives, the exercises, the exercise answers and the program at the end of each chapter all play an equally important part in the learning process. The exercises have been chosen to be a real test of a student's understanding of both concept and detail and to extend, sometimes by discovery, the knowledge and understanding gained in the narrative. Some of the exercise answers include notes on the answers which also extend a student's knowledge and understanding. A program is specified at the end of each chapter to be coded, run and tested on a computer system. Each program is designed, as far as is possible, to include the concepts contained in the chapter.

The exercises should be done when they are encountered and before continuing with the text. Additionally, the programs should at least be coded before continuing with the next chapter. Many students will be able to work through the text without assistance, allowing a tutor to concentrate his attention on those students who are unable to complete the text on their own.

The whole text is designed on the premise that one sure way to learn a programming language is by plenty of practical experience - just like learning a foreign language. Proficiency in programming is acquired by writing it. That is one reason why practical exercises have been inserted throughout the text and a program is included at the end of each chapter. The text contains many exercises which call for written answers; it is essential that the answers are written down. Eager students are sometimes tempted to answer the questions mentally in their impatience to make pogress with the subject - they should resist this temptation!

Throughout the book, modular design of assembly language programs is encouraged. To allow this, subroutines are introduced early on in the course in Chapter 3.

The text is also designed so that students can code and run programs at the earliest possible stage in a course.

At the end of each chapter there is a program specification. The program should be coded, run and tested, preferably before passsing on to the next chapter, although this may not be practicable; however, the program should at least be coded before looking at the next chapter. The program should be a fully correct working version which adheres exactly to the specification. A program is no use to anyone if it does not do exactly what is required of it.

Only one program is specified at the end of each chapter so that a student can concentrate his effort on that one program.

The programs have been carefully chosen to be stimulating and have a visual reward for success - all programs produce some form of output on a display.

If necessary, the programs can be replaced by other programs for specialist courses, although the programs in the text have been carefully chosen to cover as many aspects of Z80 assembly programming as possible.

Instead of covering all of a topic at once, most topics are spread over a few chapters and each chapter covers parts of a few topics. This allows more relevant programs to be written earlier in a course and it makes the text more interesting thereby helping a student's concentration. Additionally, because a topic is spread throughout the text, a student has time gradually to assimilate the concepts contained within a topic and to absorb each concept before proceeding to the next.

One problem encountered by tutors teaching programming languages to a group of students is the wide variation in the students' rates of learning the language - even groups of students with the same background. Consequently, a favoured method of teaching programming languages is by tutor-assisted, self-instructional methods, so that students may learn at their own rate and not become bored or lost. This text is particularly suitable for such a course.

This book is not written for use with one particular Z80 computer system - it can be used with any Z80-based microcomputer. A minimum configuration of a Z80 processor, screen and keyboard is assumed to be available for the practical programs.

This book is suitable for BSc, HND and BEC/TEC courses in computing and engineering and as a reference book for practising Z80 Assembly Language programmers.

ACKNOWLEDGEMENTS

My thanks to Leicester Polytechnic for allowing me to use their computer facilities for the development of programs and production of the book, and to Bob Reeve, of Wolverhampton Polytechnic, for his thorough checking of the text and many suggested improvements. Also, I wish to thank my wife, Susan, for her support in many ways, particularly in the typing of the text using a word processor. Thanks too to Nicolas and Elisabeth for their patience on occasions when having to wait for parental care and attention.

Roger Hutty

1   The Z80 architecture

1.1 MICROPROCESSOR SYSTEMS

Computing, like many other processes, has three main parts

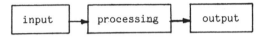

In a computer system, data (numbers and words) is input by an input device, the processing is performed by a central processing unit and data is output by an output device.

A computer system can have many different types of device but as far as a microprocessor system is concerned the most common system is shown in Figure 1.1.

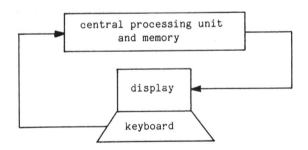

Figure 1.1

A keyboard is used to input programs, and data for the programs. A program is a list of instructions to tell the computer what to do during the processing stage. A display is used to output information, such as results from a program. The memory is used to store programs and data.

Exercise 1.1
Which input device is used in a microprocessor system and what is its purpose?

1

If you are not familiar with binary and hexadecimal number systems and signed (2's complement) and unsigned numbers you should work through Appendix A before continuing with the text.

1.2 THE Z80 CENTRAL PROCESSING UNIT

There are several different microprocessor central processing units available. This book is concerned only with the Zilog 80 (Z80) microprocessor.

* Zilog and Z80 are trademarks of Zilog, Inc., with whom the publisher is not associated. *

The components of the Z80 which are of most importance to a programmer are the registers shown in Figure 1.2.

Accumulator	A	F	Flag register
	B	C	
	D	E	
	H	L	
	SP		Stack pointer
	PC		Program counter
	IX		X index register
	IY		Y index register
		I	Interrupt vector register

Figure 1.2

The accumulator is an 8-bit register used for arithmetic and logical operations. For example, to add two numbers in the Z80 microprocessor the first number must be in the accumulator and the second number is added to the accumulator, thereby leaving the sum in the accumulator.

The flag register is used to hold information about the results of some operations. For example, the flag register indicates whether the result of adding a number to the accumulator is positive, zero or negative.

The B, C, D, E, H and L registers are often referred to as secondary registers and are used mainly to store data temporarily. They can be used as single 8-bit registers or as 16-bit registers when they are referred to as BC, DE and HL. These secondary registers tend to be used, by convention, in particular

2

ways as you will see throughout the book. In particular, the HL
register pair is usually used to point to data in memory.

The 16-bit stack pointer is used to provide a stack facility -
this will be explained later.

The 16-bit program counter is used by the central processing unit
to keep a track of the place in memory where the next instruction
to be obeyed is located.

The use of the IX and IY index registers and the interrupt vector
register will be explained later.

Exercise 1.2
Which register would you expect to be used to subtract one
number from another, and which register would you expect to
indicate whether the result is positive, zero or negative?

1.3 MEMORY

The memory of a Z80 microprocessor system consists of locations,
usually called bytes, which are 8 bits long. Look at Figure 1.3.

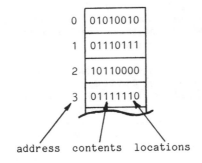

address   contents   locations

Figure 1.3

The number of bytes in a memory varies from one system to another
but will normally be 4K, 8K, 16K, 32K, 48K or 64K which are round
binary values (analogous to decimal tens and thousands, etc.). 1K
is equivalent to decimal 1024 (binary 10000000000).

Exercise 1.3
How many bytes are there in a 64K memory expressed as a decimal
number and an hexadecimal number?

The bytes of a memory are numbered sequentially starting at zero
- the number of a byte is referred to as its address. Each byte
contains an 8-bit pattern which is referred to as the contents of
the byte. The 8-bit pattern may represent any one of several
quantities such as an instruction, a number or a character.

Exercise 1.4
Referring to Figure 1.3, what is the content (in hexadecimal) of the byte whose address is 2?

A shorthand form of writing 'the content of a byte whose address is' is to enclose the address in parenthesis so that, for example, (3) is hexadecimal 7E.

In the remainder of this text binary numbers are postfixed with the letter B and hexadecimal numbers with the letter H. Numbers with no postfix letter may be assumed to be decimal.

1.4 INSTRUCTIONS

Have a quick glance at Appendix C where you will see the complete Z80 instruction set.

In general, an instruction consists of an operation and an operand. The operation indicates what has to be done and the operand indicates what is to be used in the operation. For example, the instruction

    10010010

has an operation code (op-code) of 10010B which specifies that the operand has to be 'subtracted from the accumulator' and an operand of 010B which specifies the 'contents of the register D' are to be used in the subtraction.

An instruction may occupy 1, 2, 3 or 4 bytes depending mainly on how the operand is specified. Look at the first five instructions listed in Table C.5 of Appendix C. All five instructions have an op-code of 'add to the accumulator'. Look down the column headed No. of Bytes and you will see that the number of bytes occupied by the instructions varies from one to three. This is because there are differences in the specification of the operand's address. The different ways in which an operand may be addressed are called 'addressing modes'.

Exercise 1.5
What is the instruction 'add register C to the accumulator' in binary? Use Table C.5 in Appendix C.

1.5 ASSEMBLY LANGUAGE

In the computer itself instructions are held in binary. We could write programs in binary but this would be very tedious and error-prone. We could take advantage of the hexadecimal number system and use, for example, 92H in place of the instruction 10010010B. This would be an improvement but still tedious and error-prone for any reasonably-sized program.

A more convenient way of writing programs is to use an assembly language. An assembly language has many facilities to make programming easier.

To start with, mnemonics may be used in place of operation codes. Mnemonics are usually chosen to help a programmer by indicating what the operation is. For example, the instruction referred to in the previous section, 'subtract register D from the accumulator' may be written as

SUB   D

which is easier to remember than 10010010B, or even 92H. Notice also that the operand part of the instruction, in this case register D, may be specified as the letter D in place of the code 010B.

There are many more facilities provided by the Z80 assembly language which will be introduced to you throughout the text.

Exercise 1.6
What is the assembly language instruction to 'increment register B by one'? Use Table C.5 in Appendix C.

Assembly language programs cannot be executed directly by a computer - they have to be converted to their equivalent binary codes. This conversion is performed by a program called an assembler. The assembler inputs an assembly language program, called the source program, assembles the program and produces a machine code program, called the object program, which can then be executed.

All Z80 assemblers provide the same assembly language facilities (with occasional odd exceptions). You will need to find out how to assemble and execute programs on the Z80 computer system which you intend to use for the practical programs.

2   Accumulator and register instructions

In this chapter we shall consider the one-byte operations of loading registers, adding to the accumulator, subtracting from the accumulator, incrementing and decrementing registers and negating the accumulator. All these instructions allow 8-bit arithmetic to be performed.

2.1   LOAD A REGISTER WITH A VALUE

Any of the single registers may be loaded directly with a value using the two-byte instruction

    LD   r,n

where r is any of the registers A, B, C, D, E, H or L and n is an unsigned number in the range 0 to 255 or a signed number in the range -128 to +127. For example, LD B,99 will load the B register with 99.

Exercise 2.1
Why is the range of n so specified?

2.2   ADD AND SUBTRACT A VALUE

Quantities can be added to, and subtracted from, the accumulator using the

    ADD A,n   and   SUB n

instructions, respectively. For example, the sequence of instructions

    LD   A,15
    ADD A,46
    SUB 22

will cause the accumulator to contain 15 after the LD instruction, 61 after the ADD instruction and 39 after the SUB instruction.

Notice that the ADD instruction requires the accumulator to be specified explicitly, whereas the accumulator is implied in the SUB instruction.

6

Exercise 2.2
Write a program segment which computes 73 + 55 – 21.

2.3 ADD AND SUBTRACT A REGISTER

The contents of any of the registers can be added to, or subtracted from, the accumulator using the

    ADD A,r   and   SUB r

instructions, respectively. This allows, for example, intermediate results which have been saved temporarily in one of the registers to be added to, or subtracted from, the accumulator.

2.4 LOAD ONE REGISTER WITH ANOTHER

A register may be loaded with the contents of another register with the instruction

    LD   r1,r2

which loads register r1 with the contents of register r2. This instruction is often used to save the accumulator temporarily whilst it is needed for another purpose, during which time the saved value may be used. The contents of r2 are not changed – all LD instructions perform a 'copy' rather than 'load' function.

Exercise 2.3
Write a program segment to compute 3 x (56 – 22). Do this by adding 56 – 12 twice to itself.

2.5 INCREMENT AND DECREMENT A REGISTER

The single-byte instructions

    INC r   and DEC r

increment and decrement, respectively, the register r by one. These instructions are used mainly for looping as shall be explained later. However, they can also be used to add one or subtract one during an arithmetic computation. In particular, INC A and DEC A execute faster than ADD A,1 and ADD A,–1 or SUB 1 and occupy one byte rather than two bytes of memory.

2.6 NEGATE THE ACCUMULATOR

Another single-byte instruction

    NEG

negates the accumulator. If, for example, the accumulator contains 78 and a NEG instruction is executed the accumulator will then contain –78.

Exercise 2.4
What is the content of the accumulator, in decimal and
hexadecimal, after each of the instructions in the following
program segment?

```
LD   A,27
NEG
INC  A
```

2.7 ADDRESSING MODES - IMMEDIATE AND EXTENDED

The three instructions LD r,n, ADD A,n and SUB n are using the
immediate addressing mode - so called because the value of the
operand is included in the instruction (in the second byte for
these particular instructions).

Another addressing mode - extended addressing - allows the
address of the operand to be specified. For example,

```
LD   A,(127AH)
```

specifies that the contents of byte 127AH are to be loaded into
the accumulator. Conversely, the contents of the accumulator can
be stored in a byte using the instruction

```
LD   (nn),A
```

where nn is the address of the byte in which the contents of the
accumulator are to be stored.

These two instructions occupy three bytes - the address of the
operand nn occupies the last two bytes of the instruction.

Exercise 2.5
Assuming byte 35H contains 79, what will be the contents of the
accumulator after the instructions

```
i)   LD   A,35H     and     ii)   LD   A,(35H)
```

have been executed?

By looking at Table C.2 in Appendix C you will see that, of the
single registers, only the accumulator may be loaded and stored
using the extended addressing mode.

2.8 LABELS

Keeping track of addresses in a program can be quite difficult.
The assembler overcomes this difficulty by allowing bytes in
memory to be given labels - analogous to giving a house a name.
A labelled byte may then be referred to by its label rather than
its address number. Only those bytes to which a reference is
made are labelled, as shown in Program 2.1 which adds 10 to a
number.

```
                    ; Program 2.1  adds 10 to a number
                    ;
0000   3A0900               LD    A,(NUMBER)
0003   C60A                 ADD   A,10
0005   320A00               LD    (RESULT),A  ; result = number + 10
0008   76                   HALT
0009   4A           NUMBER: DEFB 74
000A   00           RESULT: DEFB 0
```

Labels are chosen by a programmer within the constraints that
they must consist of no more than six letters and digits, the
first of which must be a letter. A label is terminated by the
colon character. Careful thought in choosing labels can produce
intelligible programs as shown in Program 2.1. No thought can
produce really 'bad' programs.

Program 2.1 shows the listing produced by the assembler after the
source program has been assembled. The first column of the
assembler listing gives the byte address of an instruction or
data byte and the second column is the object program, in
hexadecimal.

The listing shows how the assembler has assigned values - their
byte address number - to the labels. For example, NUMBER has the
value 9H.

The HALT instruction causes the program to stop executing.

The DEFB pseudo operator requests the assembler to allocate a
byte and set it to the specified number. Pseudo operators will be
dealt with in more detail later in the text.

Comments should always be included in assembly language programs
to make their function intelligible to a human reader. As shown
in Program 2.1 comments start with a semi-colon. The assembler
ignores all characters after a semi-colon in a line during
assembly but includes them in the listing. Comments may start at
any position in a line, including the beginning of a line. It is
difficult to define the level of comments - certainly, the level
should be higher than a comment beside each instruction. Looking
at the comments in the programs throughout the text will give you
a good idea of the level required.

2.9 PROGRAM

Write a program which computes

    RESULT = N1 - 3(N2 + 1) - 1

Set up N1 and N2 and RESULT as data at the end of your program.
When supplying values for the variables ensure that all results,
intermediate and final, will be in the range -128 to 127.

Enter the program in the computer and have it assembled and

executed. Check the computation by looking at the contents of the byte RESULT. Find out from your tutor how to look at the contents of bytes.

To see what is happening during execution of your program, single-step through the program looking at the contents of the registers and relevant bytes after the execution of each instruction. Find out from your tutor how to single-step through a program.

Change the values of N1 and N2 and repeat the assembly, execution, checking and single-stepping of your program.

3   Subroutines and display output

3.1   SUBROUTINE CONCEPTS

Subroutines are a very important feature of programming which, unfortunately, are usually left until the end of a programming course. At this stage in the book you will learn why subroutines are used and how to use them, but not how they work. The subroutine mechanism will be covered in a Chapter 7.

Let us first look at the reason for using subroutines. Suppose a program contains two or more groups of statements which are functionally identical, as indicated by the shaded areas on the left of Figure 3.1.

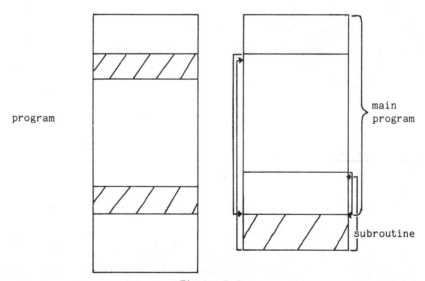

program

main program

subroutine

Figure 3.1

It is wasteful to repeat the statements, so instead we make the group of statements into a subroutine as shown on the right of Figure 3.1. The program now consists of a main program followed by the subroutine. In the main program, when the group of

statements is required to be executed, a reference is made to the
subroutine, the group of statements is executed and return is
made to the main program. Execution then continues normally in
the main program until a further reference is made to the
subroutine.

An important point to notice is that references from the main
program are made to the same place (the start of a subroutine)
but returns to the main program are made to different places in
the main program (following the reference). The mechanism for
returning to the correct place in the main program will be dealt
with later. When a main program makes a reference to a
subroutine we say that it is calling the subroutine.

3.2 THE CALL AND RET INSTRUCTIONS

Subroutines are called in the Z80 microprocessor by using the
CALL instruction followed by a label which is the label of the
first instruction of the subroutine. Program 3.1 shows a
subroutine being called twice from a main program.

```
        ; Program 3.1 multiplies two numbers by 4
        ;
                LD    A,(N1)     ; start of main program
                CALL  QUAD       ; compute N1 x 4
                LD    (R1),A     ; R1 = N1 x 4
        ;
                LD    A,(N2)
                CALL  QUAD
                LD    (R2),A     ; R2 = N2 x 4
                HALT
N1:             DEFB 31
N2:             DEFB 25
R1:             DEFB 0
R2:             DEFB 0
        ;
        ; Subroutine - multiplies the accumulator by 4
        ;
QUAD:           ADD   A,A        ; A x 2
                ADD   A,A        ; (A x 2) x 2 = A x 4
                RET
```

The subroutine, referred to by its label as QUAD, multiplies the
number in the accumulator by four.

Going through the program as it would be executed, first the
accumulator is loaded with N1 and then the subroutine QUAD is
called with the CALL QUAD instruction. This causes the
subroutine's first instruction ADD A,A to be executed, followed
by the second instruction ADD A,A. The last instruction in the
subroutine, RET, is used to return to the main program - to the
LD (R1),A instruction in this case.

The main program then continues its execution with the LD A,(N2)
instruction which loads the accumulator with N2 before calling

the subroutine again with the second CALL QUAD instruction. The subroutine's two ADD instructions will be executed, followed by the RET instruction which causes a return to the main program – to the LD (R2),A instruction this time. Finally, the program terminates with the HALT instruction.

The accumulator is being used by the QUAD subroutine to accept data – the number to be quadrupled – from the main program and to return data – the number quadrupled to the main program. We say that the accumulator is being used to 'pass parameters' to and from the subroutine, the parameters in this case being the number and the number quadrupled. Other registers, memory bytes and the stack may also be used to pass parameters as we shall see later.

Exercise 3.1
Write a subroutine which sums the contents of the registers B, C, D, E, H and L and leaves the result in the accumulator; write an associated main program which calls the subroutine.

A main program may need to use more than one subroutine. In that case, all the required subroutines are located at the end of the main program, one after the other.

3.3   DISPLAY OUTPUT

One advantage of subroutines is that a programmer can use someone else's subroutine without necessarily knowing how the subroutine performs its function.

You would usually have to go further than the third chapter in an assembly language programming book to learn how to output to the display.   However, if you are given a subroutine which performs that function and told how to use it, it does not matter that you do not understand what is going on inside the subroutine.

A subroutine to output a character to the display is given in Program 3.2.

```
; Program 3.2
;
; Subroutine to output a character to the display
;  –on entry the accumulator contains the code of the
;   character to be output
;
COUT:   PUSH AF        ; save A
INSTAT: IN   A,(ODFH)  ; read display status
        BIT  0,A        ; display ready?
        JR   Z,INSTAT  ; no – try again
        POP  AF         ; yes – restore A
        OUT  (ODEH),A  ; output character
        RET             ; return to calling program
```

The subroutine is called by the instruction CALL COUT after ensuring that the code of the character to be output is in the accumulator.   Incidentally, the character code is still in the accumulator on return from the subroutine.

The ASCII character codes are given in Appendix D. A character's ASCII code is the binary pattern which is used when transmitting a character from the cpu to a device and vice versa.

Exercise 3.2
What is the ASCII code for the character G and which character has an ASCII code of 2BH?

A character code can be specified in a program by writing either the numeric equivalent of the code or the character between apostrophes. For example, LD A,2AH and LD A,'*' can both be used to load the accumulator with the ASCII code of the * character. The latter form is preferable because it is more understandable - the assembler does the work of converting it into its numeric equivalent.

3.4 PSEUDO OPERATIONS

Pseudo operations are so-called because, although they appear in an assembly language program in the same place as the operator of an executable instructions, they are not executed - not even assembled. In fact, pseudo operations are information provide by the programmer for the assembler. We have already used one pseudo operator - the DEFB pseudo operator which informs the assembler that a byte and its contents are being defined.

There are several other pseudo operators which will be introduced throughout the text. For now, we will look at two little-used pseudo operators.

The ORG nn pseudo operator informs the assembler that the followinginstruction is to be assembled so that it starts at address nn. The mnemonic ORG, which is short for ORiGin, was chosen because this pseudo operator is mainly used to indicate the address of the start of a program, although it can be used anywhere within a program. The ORG pseudo operator allows a programmer to specify the absolute address of the place in memory where a program is to reside. However, most microprocessors are used under the control of an operating system, such as CP/M (Control Program / Monitor), which either controls the allocation of memory to programs or allows a program to be located at an absolute place after the assembly of the program - usually during the linking phase. Hence, it is now standard practice for an assembler always to assemble a program relative to byte zero, and the ORG pseudo operator has gone out of use.

Exercise 3.3
Referring to Program 2.1, if the first instruction was preceded by the pseudo operation ORG 1000H what would be the address of the byte occupied by the HALT instruction?

The END pseudo operator has also now gone out of general use.Its function is to inform the assembler that there is no more program to assemble, that is, to indicate the end of a program. This is necessary in some environments, such as the old paper-tape systems, where it is not clear that the end of the program has been reached. However, programs are now more normally held in files, of one kind or another, and the assembler automatically finds the end of a program by detecting the end of the file containing the program. Purists would say that a program should always finish with the END pseudo operator but since it is usually obvious where the end of a program is, it is now rarely used. Exceptionally, some assembler systems require programs to be terminated with an END pseudo operator.

3.5 PROGRAM

Using the COUT subroutine write a program which outputs your initials followed by a carriage-return and line-feed (referred to as CR and LF in the ASCII character codes in Appendix D).

Note: You must check with your tutor or computer supplier that the display output subroutine is correct in every detail for your particular Z80 computer system. The addresses DFH and DEH may well be different and, in fact, the whole subroutine may be quite different, particularly if your system uses memory-mapped output. Also, you should check with your tutor or computer supplier to see if the stack needs to be initialised at the start of your program. Most operating systems do this job for you.

4 Unconditional jumps and keyboard input

4.1 UNCONDITIONAL JUMPS

Execution of Z80 programs we have looked at so far proceeds sequentially through the instructions, one after another. However, it is possible and, in fact, usual to change the sequence of execution for one reason or another. Jump instructions allow the execution of a program to take different paths through the instructions. There are two types of jump instructions - unconditional and conditional. We will look at conditional jumps in the next chapter.

An unconditional jump has the form

        JP   nn

where nn is the address of a memory byte. The instruction will cause the instruction at address nn to be executed after the JP instruction. The address is normally specified as the label of the instruction to be jumped to, rather than its actual address.

Without conditional jumps the use of the JP instruction is limited to providing indefinite loops, as shown in Program 4.1.

```
; Program 4.1  an indefinite loop
          -                 ; initial part of program
          -
LOOP:     -                 ; *
          -                 ; * instructions to be repeated
          -                 ; *
          JP    LOOP        ; jump to LOOP
```

The initial part of the program will be executed first, followed by the instructions to be repeated. Then the JP LOOP instruction causes a jump to the first instruction of those to be repeated. The remainder of the instructions in the loop will be executed until the JP LOOP is executed again, and so on.

The programming of indefinite loops is not recommended because the only way to stop the looping is to 'crash' the system by pressing the RESET button or worse, switching off the computer. Use of conditional jumps prevents the need to code indefinite loops, as we shall see in the next chapter.

Exercise 4.1
Write a set of instructions which repeatedly outputs an asterisk
character to the display.

The JP instruction allows a jump to be made to any instruction in
a memory of 64K bytes. However, because most jumps are to
instructions within a few bytes from the jump instruction a
shorter version, the JR instruction, is also available. The JR
mnemonic stands for 'Jump Relative', so-called because the
address part of the instruction specifies the number of bytes
between the JR instruction and the instruction to which the jump
is to be made.

Exercise 4.2
Using Table C.10 in Appendix C determine how many bytes are
occupied by a JP instruction and a JR instruction.

4.2   KEYBOARD INPUT

In the same way that you were given a subroutine to output to the
display you are now given a subroutine called CIN which accepts a
character from the keyboard.   The subroutine is shown in Program
4.2.

```
; Program 4.2
;
; Subroutine to input a character from the keyboad
;      -on return the accumulator contains the code of the
;       character
;
CIN:    IN    A,(0DFH)   ; has key
        BIT   1,A        ; been pressed?
        JR    Z,CIN      ; no - try again
        IN    A,(0DEH)   ; yes - input character
        RET              ; return to calling program
```

On return from the subroutine, the accumulator contains the ASCII
code of the character which was input from the keyboard.   The
subroutine is called by the instruction CALL CIN.

A character which is input from the keyboard is not normally
automatically displayed on the display unit.   To display, or echo
as is normally said, a character which has been input from the
keyboard, it must immediately be output.

Exercise 4.3
Knowing that a subroutine can call another subroutine, which can
call another subroutine, and so on, write a subroutine called
CINEKO which inputs a character from the keyboard and echoes it
on the display.

You should check with your tutor or computer supplier that the
input subroutine in Program 4.2 is correct, in every detail, for

your particular computer system. You will also need to check if an input character is automatically echoed, or not.

Groups of statements which are required more then once in a program or which are likely to be required by more than one program should be made into a subroutine. The program you had to write in Chapter 3 required a carriage-return and line-feed to be output to the display. This is obviously going to be a common requirement in many programs which affect the display. It is prudent, therefore, to make the group of statements which perform that function into a subroutine called CRLF, which can then be called from a program by the instruction CALL CRLF whenever a carriage-return and a line-feed is required to be output.

This approach to programming is referred to as modular programming, or more precisely modular design. Although normally associated with high-level language programming, it is a desirable feature of assembly language programming because it saves time when a program is originated and also reduces subsequent maintenance times associated with a program.

4.3 CHARACTER CODES AND VALUES

You must be careful when working with digits that you do not confuse a digit's character code with its value. The two are quite different.

The values of the digits 0 to 9 are represented in registers and memory bytes in the computer by the numbers 00H to 09H.

The character codes of the digits 0 to 9 are represented by the numbers 30H to 39H.

The values of digits are used when doing arithmetic in the computer and the character codes of digits are used during input and output of digital characters. The character code of a digit which is input and needs to be used in arithmetic must be converted to the value of the digit, and vice versa.

Exercise 4.4
What is the content of the accumulator after the execution of the instructions

     LD   A,'7'   and   LD   A,8

4.4   THE EQU PSEUDO OPERATOR

The EQU pseudo operator is a little-used pseudo operator which should be used more often. It allows a programmer to give a constant a name by assigning a value to a label. Its main advantages are that it makes a program more readable and easier to change for different environments. For example, when loading the accumulator with the carriage-return character code, it is more obvious what is being done if

18

```
  CR:       EQU  13
            —
            —
            LD   A,CR
```

is used. The EQU (short for EQUate) pseudo operator normally
occurs at the beginning of a program. A label may only be equated
once, but may be used as many times as necessary once it has been
defined.

Another example of the EQU pseudo operator being put to good use
is the naming of the addresses of the display and keyboard status
and data bytes. The outline of a program using the display and
keyboard would look like

```
  DATA:    EQU  ODEH
  STATUS:  EQU  ODFH


  CIN:     IN   A,(STATUS)
           —
           IN   A,(DATA)
           —
  COUT:    PUSH AF
  INSTAT:  IN   A,(STATUS)
           —
           OUT  (DATA),A
           —
```

Now, if it is necessary to change the staus and data byte
addresses, only the two EQU pseudo operators at the beginning of
the program need be amended and the program re-assembled.

In general, all numbers in a program which represent a code or an
address should be equated. This does not include numbers which
are to be used for the value which they represent.

4.5 PROGRAM

Write a program which repeatedly inputs (and echoes) two decimal
digits from the keyboard and outputs their sum. It may be
assumed that the sum of the two digits does not exceed 9. A
typical run of the program would leave the display containing

```
  2+2=4
  5+3=8
  4+1=5
```

It is the program's responsibility to output the + and =
characters.

There is usually no need to rewrite a subroutine each time it is
required by a program. Each subroutine can be set up in a file
of its own so that whenever it needs to be appended at the end of

the main program just a single statement in the program, such as
*INCLUDE subroutine-file-name, will cause the subroutine to be
included. The precise method of providing this facility varies
from one system to another, so ask your tutor or computer
supplier how it can be done - it will save you a great deal of
time.

5 Flags, conditional jumps and the CP instruction

5.1 THE FLAG REGISTER

The Z80 has an 8-bit flag register which is used to contain information regarding the result produced by the last executed instruction. In fact, only six of the eight bits are used as follows

S	Z	X	H	X	P/V	N	C

S   - Sign flag
Z   - Zero flag
H   - Half-carry flag
P/V - Parity/Overflow flag
N   - Add/Subtract flag
C   - Carry flag
X   - Unused bits

The SIGN FLAG is set to 1 if the result produced by an instruction is negative, otherwise the flag is reset to 0. For example, after execution of the instructions

        LD   A,23
        SUB   56

the accumulator will contain -33 and the sign flag will be set to 1.

The ZERO FLAG is set to 1 if the result produced by an instruction is zero, otherwise the flag is reset to 0. The zero flag would be reset to 0 after the execution of the two instructions above.

The operation of the S and Z flags will suffice for now - the H, P/V, N and C flags will be dealt with later in the book.

Not all instructions affect all of the flags. For example, none of the LD instructions affects any flags. You can discover which instructions affect which flags by looking in the third column of the tables in Appendix C. Glancing through the tables you will

see that the sign and zero flags are mainly affected by
arithmetic, shift, rotate and bit instructions.

Exercise 5.1
Give the contents of the accumulator and the S and Z flags after
execution of each of the following instructions

```
LD    A,120
SUB   122
LD    B,A
SUB   B
ADD   A,70
NEG
```

We shall now look at conditional jump instructions which use the
flag bits.

5.2   CONDITIONAL JUMP INSTRUCTIONS

Conditional jump instructions allow a program either to continue
executing the instructions following the instruction or to
execute a set of instructions elsewhere in the program, depending
on the state of one of the flag bits. This allows a program to
go one way or another depending on a condition. A conditional
jump instruction is used in Program 5.1.

```
; Program 5.1
;
            LD    A,(X)
            SUB   10        ; compute X-10
            JP    Z,EQUAL
            LD    A,1        ; X ≠ 10
            JP    CONTIN
EQUAL:      LD    A,0        ; X = 10
CONTIN: -
          -
X:          DEFB  25
```

The program resets the accumulator to 0 if X is equal to 10 or
sets it to 1 if X is not equal to 10. The SUB instruction
computes X - 10 and sets the sign and zero flags according to the
result of that computation. With X having a value of 25, both
the sign and zero flags will be reset to 0.

The JP Z,EQUAL instruction causes a jump to the instruction
labelled EQUAL if the zero flag is 1, or execution of the
following instruction, LD A,1, if the zero flag is 0. With X
having a value of 25, no jump will be made, and the LD A,1
instruction will be executed followed by the unconditional jump
instruction JP CONTIN.

Exercise 5.2
Referring to Program 5.1, give the order of execution of
instructions if the value of X had been defined as 10.

22

Four of the conditions which can be tested by a conditional jump instruction are

```
Zero      -  jump if zero flag is 1  -  eg.  JP  Z,EQUAL
Non Zero  -  jump if zero flag is 0  -  eg.  JP  NZ,DIFF
Minus     -  jump if sign flag is 1  -  eg.  JP  M,NEG
Positive  -  jump if sign flag is 0  -  eg.  JP  P,POS
```

Exercise 5.3
Write a program segment which outputs the letter N if the sum of two numbers which are in the B and C registers, is negative, the letter Z if the sum is zero or the letter P if the sum is positive, but not zero.

The JP Z and JP NZ have equivalent relative jump instructions JR Z and JR NZ in the same way as the unconditional JP instruction has an equivalent JR instruction. The JP M and JP P instructions do not have relative equivalents.

5.3 THE COMPARE INSTRUCTION

The Z80 compare instruction is very useful because it allows the accumulator to be compared with another value without affecting the contents of the accumulator as, for example, do the SUB and ADD instructions. The compare instruction computes the value of the operand subtracted from the accumulator and sets the flags according to the result of the computation. The result does NOT replace the contents of the accumulator – the result is discarded. The instruction has a mnemonic of CP and can have an operand of a register or an 8-bit value.

The most straightforward use of the CP instruction is determining if the accumulator contains a specific value or not. For example, the instructions

```
CP   50
JR   Z,FIFTY
```

will cause the Z flag to be set to 1 if the accumulator contains 50 and reset to 0 otherwise, followed by a jump to the instruction labelled FIFTY if, in fact, the accumulator does contain 50.

Exercise 5.4
Write a program segment which causes a jump to an instruction labelled LESS if the value of a variable COUNT is less than 100, to an instruction labelled EQUAL if COUNT is equal to 100 or to an instruction labelled GREAT if COUNT is greater than 100.

The CP 0 instruction is useful for setting the flag register after an instruction which does not affect the flags. For example, the LD instruction in the sequence

```
LD   A,(TEMP)
CP   0
```

does not affect the flags and a CP 0 instruction is, therefore, necessary if the status of the accumulator is required.

5.4 CONDITIONAL LOOP TERMINATION

The loops which were considered in the previous chapter were referred to as indefinite loops because there were no instructions to stop the looping.

We shall be considering several different methods of terminating loops in subsequent chapters, but for now we shall consider just one method in which the loop is terminated when a specified condition occurs. Program 5.2 contains a loop which inputs characters until a blank character is input.

```
        ; Program 5.2
        ;
NEXTCH: CALL  CINEKO
        CP    ' '
        JP    NZ,NEXTCH
NOBLK:  -
        -
```

The three instructions in the program will be repeatedly executed until the character input is the blank character. When this occurs, the CP instruction will produce a zero result causing the instruction following the JP NZ,NEXTCH instruction to be executed next rather than the instruction labelled NEXTCH.

5.5 PROGRAM

First write a subroutine to categorise a character code. On entry to the subroutine the accumulator contains the character code. The subroutine returns with the accumulator unchanged and register B containing

      -1 if the character is a decimal digit,
       0 if the character is a letter of the alphabet (small and capital),
 or 1 otherwise.

You will need to consult the table of character codes in Appendix D.

Use the subroutine to write a main program which repeatedly inputs a character from the keyboard and responds, after outputting a space, by displaying the letter D, A or N indicating that the character just input was a decimal digit, an alphabetic character or neither, respectively. The letter should be followed by a carriage-return and line-feed.

Pressing the RETURN key should terminate the program.

6 Counting loops and the stack

There are many different constructions used in looping. We have already used an 'indefinite loop' construct (not recommended) and a 'conditional terminated loop' construct. We shall consider several more types of loop construct throughout the book, starting now with a 'counting loop' construct.

6.1 COUNTING LOOPS

One of the simplest loop constructions allows a sequence of instructions to be executed n times. An example of this is shown in Program 6.1 which inputs 10 digits and sums them.

```
; Program 6.1 input and sum 10 numbers
;
          LD   C,0      ; C contains running sum
          LD   B,10     ; initialise loop counter
NEXT:     CALL CINEKO   ; input digit
          SUB  30H      ; convert digit to its value
          ADD  A,C      ; add digit to running sum
          LD   C,A
          DJNZ NEXT
CONTIN: -
```

The sequence of instructions between, and including, CALL CINEKO and LD C,A will be executed 10 times. The loop counter, register B in this example, is initially loaded with the number of times that the loop is to be executed using the LD B,10 instruction. The DJNZ (Decrement and Jump on Non Zero) instruction causes register B to be decremented and a jump made to the specified label NEXT if B is not zero. When B does become zero, after the loop instructions have been executed 10 times, execution will continue with the instruction following the DJNZ instruction, that is, the one labelled CONTIN.

Exercise 6.1
What is the maximum loop count that can be used by the loop construction in Program 6.1?

It is not good programming practice to write specialised programs like, for example, Program 6.1 which has been written for a fixed

25

loop count of 10. Normally, programs are written to be of
general use, although not so general that it is difficult to use
a program for a particular case. For counting loops the initial
value of the loop counter can be a parameter of a subroutine if
the loop is contained in a subroutine, a value input from the
keyboard, or a value computed prior to the loop.

Exercise 6.2
Write a program which inputs a digit n from the keyboard and
displays n asterisks.

Other registers, and memory bytes, can be used as the loop
counter as well as the B register. The reason why the B register
is a first choice is because of the DJNZ instruction. However,
this instruction applies to the B register only. A counting loop
using, for example, the accumulator looks like

```
              -
              LD    A,initial-value
     NEXT:    -
              -
              DEC   A
              JR    NZ,NEXT
              -
```

which requires two separate instructions to decrement and test
the accumulator. Hence, DEC B followed by JR NZ,label is
equivalent to DJNZ label.

It is sometimes convenient to use the loop counter within the
sequence of instructions to be repeated. Suppose, for example,
we wanted to sum the numbers from 1 to n.

Program 6.2 does just that by adding in the loop counter, which
goes from n to 1, each time through the loop.

```
     ; Program 6.2   sum the numbers 1 to n
     ;
     N:       EQU   11
              LD    A,0       ; set sum to 0
              LD    B,N
     NEXADD:  ADD   A,B       ; add n to sum
              DJNZ  NEXADD
              -
```

The loop counter is being used to count the number of times that
the sequence of instructions is executed and also as the value to
be added in each time round through the loop. After looping is
complete the accumulator will contain the sum. Notice that the
accumulator must be set to zero to start with.

When the loop counter is being used within a repeated sequence of
instructions it is not always convenient to count down to 0. If
the lower value is not zero then a compare instruction must be
used to detect the end of looping. As the compare instruction

operates only on the accumulator, this technique implies the use of the accumulator as the loop counter.

Exercise 6.3
Write a program which outputs the decimal digits 9 to 0, in descending order.

6.2   NUMBER INPUT

So far we have only considered the input of a single digit number from the keyboard. Inputting a number with more than one digit is not so straightforward.

If, for example, we wanted to input the number 123 it would have to be input as three separate digits - the digit 1 followed by the digit 2 followed by the digit 3. This would be done with three CALLs to the CINEKO subroutine so the program would then have the character codes for the three digits 1, 2 and 3. How then do we convert these codes to form the 8-bit value 123 in a register or memory byte?

First of all each digit's character code must be converted to the digit's value. Then the first digit's value is multiplied by 100, the second digit's value is multiplied by 10 and these two products are added to the third digit's value to give the total value of the number. So that for the number 123 the computation

    1 x 100 + 2 x 10 + 3

would be performed.

An equivalent, but more efficient, algorithm for computing the value of a 3-digit number is

    ((first digit x 10) + second digit) x 10 + last digit

which can easily be extended to an algorithm which inputs an n-digit number.

6.3   THE STACK

The Z80 stack is an area of memory in which a stack facility exists. The main characteristic of a stack is that items may only be added to, and removed from, the top of the stack. A stack is also referred to as a LIFO (Last-In-First-Out) queue. Figure 6.1 shows how a Z80 stack is organised.

A stack has a top and a bottom. The bottom of the stack is where the first item was added to the stack and the top of the stack is where the last item was added. (A Z80 stack item is two bytes.) The stack pointer (SP) register always points to the top of the stack. Initially, when the stack is empty, the stack pointer points to just below the bottom of the stack.

27

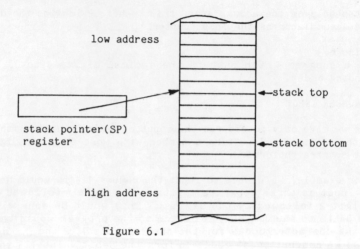

low address

stack pointer(SP) register

←stack top

←stack bottom

high address

Figure 6.1

You can see from Figure 6.1 that the stack bottom is a high address and the top is a low address, so usually the stack bottom is a memory byte with one of the highest addresses. The address of the stack bottom can be set by program instructions and there may be more than one stack. However, a system will usually have only one stack and the address of that stack bottom will be set by the operating system.

Items may be added to the stack, or pushed on the stack, as we say, when the SP register will be decremented by two to point to the new top of the stack. Also, items may be removed from the stack, or popped off, as we say, when the SP register will be incremented by two to point to the new top of the stack.

The stack is used mainly for the temporary storage of data and addresses, an example of which we shall look at in the next section and also in the subroutine mechanism which will be discussed in the next chapter.

6.4   THE STACK INSTRUCTIONS

The stack bottom can be initialised using one of several instructions which load the SP register with a value.

The two most commonly used of these instructions are LD SP,value and LD SP,(label). So, for example, LD SP,32767 will set the bottom of the stack to the byte with address 32767.

Having initialised the stack, items may be pushed on the stack and popped off the stack. Only the contents of the register pairs AF, BC, DE, HL, IX and IY may be pushed on and popped off the stack, so for any operation on the stack, its size increases or decreases by two bytes. The two instructions for popping and pushing are POP rp and PUSH rp, where rp is any one of the register pairs listed above. When a register pair has been PUSHed on to the stack the contents of the SP register are decremented by two to point to the new top of the stack, and when a register pair has been POPped off the stack the contents of the SP register are incremented by two.

Exercise 6.4
What will be the contents of the registers A, B, C, D, E and SP after execution of the following program segment?

```
        LD   A,0AH
        LD   B,0BH
        LD   C,0CH
        LD   D,0DH
        LD   E,0EH
        LD   SP,16383
        PUSH AF
        PUSH BC
        PUSH DE
        POP  BC
        POP  DE
```

Another useful stack instruction is EX (SP),HL which exchanges the top of the stack with the contents of the HL register pair. The exchange may take place also with the IX and IY registers using the EX (SP),IX and EX (SP),IY instructions, respectively.

6.5   SAVING AND RESTORING REGISTERS

A subroutine should normally leave all registers in the state that it finds them, except those which are used to pass parameters back to the main program or calling subroutine. The technique for doing this is referred to as 'saving and restoring registers'. On entry to the subroutine, the subroutine saves any registers that it is going to use and then restores those registers just before returning. The simplest method of saving and restoring registers uses the stack. For example, if a subroutine uses registers B, C and D, then the start and end of the subroutine would look like

```
  SUBIN:  PUSH BC
          PUSH DE
          -
          -
          POP  DE
          POP  BC
          RET
```

When using the stack in this way care must be taken to ensure that registers placed on the stack are removed before the RET instruction and also that the registers are POPed off in reverse order.

When a subroutine does not save used registers, there should be a comment at the beginning of the subroutine indicating which registers are affected by the subroutine.

6.6 PROGRAM

Repeated addition can be used as a crude method of multiplying two numbers since, for example, 3 x 4 is equivalent to 3 + 3 + 3 + 3. So, to multiply p by q, p is added to itself q - 1 times.

Write a subroutine called MULT which multiplies the B register by the C register and leaves the product in the accumulator. The subroutine may assume that the resulting product is not too large to be contained in the accumulator.

Write a subroutine called NUMIN which inputs an unsigned decimal number consisting of any number of digits. The number is terminated by any non-digit character and may have leading spaces which are ignored by the subroutine. On return from the subroutine the accumulator should contain the number and the B register should contain the number of digits in the number.

Use the MULT and NUMIN subroutines, and subroutines from previous programs, to write a main program which repeatedly inputs (with echo) a decimal number terminated by a comma and outputs either the word OK if the number contains two digits (leading zeros included) other than 99, or the number of digits, otherwise.

One advantage of modular programming is that a module - a subroutine in assembly language programming - can be replaced by another module without affecting the rest of the program provided that the new module performs exactly the same function as the old module and that parameters are passed in the same way. For example, when you are able to write a 'better' multiply subroutine, the crude one you have used in this program can simply be replaced, without affecting any program which uses the subroutine.

7 Nested loops and addressing modes

7.1 NESTED LOOPS

A natural extension of the loops we have used so far is a construction which has a loop within a loop, within a loop, and so on. This type of construction is referred to as nested loops, because each loop nests insides another loop. The terms outer loop and inner loop are used to describe a loop containing another loop, and a loop which is inside another loop, respectively. Program 7.1 shows a program with two loops.

```
; Program 7.1   outputs 4 lines of 6 *'s
;
        LD   C,4        ; initialise line count
NEXTC:  CALL CRLF       ; line loop start
        LD   A,'*'
        LD   B,6        ; initialise * count
NEXTB:  CALL COUT       ; * loop start
        DJNZ NEXTB      ; * loop end
        DEC  C
        JP   NZ,NEXTC   ; line loop end
        HALT
```

The program outputs four lines of six asterisks. The outer loop uses the C register to count the number of lines and the inner loop uses the B register to count the number of asterisks.

Exercise 7.1
During the complete execution of Program 7.1 how many times will each of the instructions LD A,'*', CALL COUT and DEC C be executed?

Although Program 7.1 shows two standard counting loops, there may be more than two loops nested and any one of the nested loops may be any type of loop which is used in any way and terminated in any way.

7.2 IMMEDIATE EXTENDED AND REGISTER INDIRECT ADDRESSING MODES

The Z80 microprocessor has ten addressing modes, that is, ten different ways of specifying the operand of an instruction. We have already looked at two addressing modes explicitly (immediate and extended), but have used another three (register, implied and relative) without special mention.

31

Immediate addressing mode has the value of the operand included in the instruction - in the second byte.

Extended addressing mode has the address of the operand included in the instruction.

Register addressing mode has one of the registers as the operand.

Implied addressing mode has the operand implied, that is, not explicitly stated in the instruction.

Relative addressing mode is the one in which the instruction contains a relative displacement between a jump instruction and the instruction to which the jump is to be made, such as the JR conditional and unconditional jump instructions.

Figure 7.1 compares the immediate and extended addressing modes.

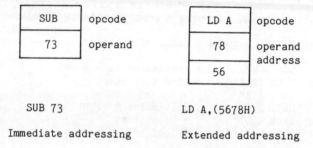

SUB 73   LD A,(5678H)

Immediate addressing   Extended addressing

Figure 7.1

Exercise 7.2
Which addressing mode is being used by the following instructions?

    i)   NEG
   ii)   INC D
  iii)   CP   50
   iv)   LD   A,(6352H)

We shall now consider two more addressing modes - register indirect and immediate extended.

Immediate extended addressing mode is, as its name suggests, an extension of the immediate addressing mode. Immediate addressing refers to 8-bit values whereas immediate extended refers to 16-bit values.

In the immediate extended addressing mode the operand is the 16-bit value in the last two bytes of the instruction. For example, the instruction LD BC,4985 would cause the register pair BC to be loaded with the value 4985. The three register pairs BC, DE and HL may all be loaded with a value, although you will find that the register pair HL is the most used in this way because that pair is used to point to data following the end of a program. To use the data in the program it is first necessary for HL to contain the address of the data as follows

```
        LD    HL,NUMBER
              -
              -
NUMBER: DEFB -25
```

The instruction LD HL,NUMBER causes the address of the data byte labelled NUMBER to be loaded into the HL register pair.

In register indirect addressing mode, the address of the operand is contained in a register pair, so that, for example, the instruction LD A,(HL) causes the accumulator to be loaded with the contents of the memory byte whose address is in HL.

Figure 7.2 compares the immediate extended and register indirect addressing modes.

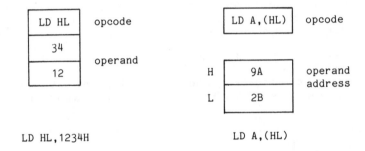

        LD HL,1234H   LD A,(HL)

    Immediate extended addressing   Register indirect addressing

Figure 7.2

The register indirect addressing mode can be used in addition - ADD A,(HL) - and subtraction - SUB (HL). Also, a memory byte may be loaded from the accumulator using this addressing mode - LD (HL),A.

Program 7.2 shows the use of the immediate extended and register indirect addressing modes.

The program computes the sum and the difference of two numbers N1 and N2 which are located in a data area at the end of the program.

The first instruction in the program sets HL to point to the data byte N2. With N1 in the accumulator, the SUB (HL) instruction causes the contents of the memory byte pointed to by HL, to be subtracted from the accumulator. Similarly, the ADD A,(HL) instruction causes the contents of N2 to be added to the accumulator.

33

```
; Program 7.2  sum  and difference of 2 numbers
;
            LD    HL,N2        ; HL points to N2
;
            LD    A,(N1)
            SUB   (HL)         ; DIFF = N1 - N2
            LD    (DIFF),A
            LD    A,(N1)
            ADD   A,(HL)       ; SUM = N1 + N2
            LD    (SUM),A
            HALT
;
N1:         DEFB  14H
N2:         DEFB  -23H
DIFF:       DEFB  0
SUM:        DEFB  0
```

Exercise 7.3
If the address of memory byte N1 is 1760H, what will be the
contents of the accumulator and the HL register pair after
execution of each of the instructions in Program 7.2?

7.3   THE DEFM PSEUDO OPERATOR

A string of characters can be specified in the data area of a
program by using several DEFB psueudo operators, as follows

```
    TEXT:   DEFB  'M'
            DEFB  'E'
            DEFB  'S'
            DEFB  'S'
            DEFB  'A'
            DEFB  'G'
            DEFB  'E'
```

However, that is rather tedious and unnecessary because

```
    TEXT:   DEFM  'MESSAGE'
```

is exactly equivalent to the seven DEFBs above but is quicker to
write and easier to read and understand. On detecting a DEFM
pseudo operator the assembler puts the first character, M in this
case, in the memory byte labelled TEXT and the remaining
characters in order in the next six bytes.

The pseudo operator DEFM actually stands for DEFine Message.

Exercise 7.4
Write a character string labelled MESS12 which would appear as

    FIRST LINE
    SECOND LINE

when output to the display.

7.4   TEXT OUTPUT

When only one, two or three characters are being output to the display it is normal to output them with separate sets of statements, each of which loads the accumulator with a character and calls COUT. However, for three or more characters this would be a very inefficient way to output them to the display.

A more efficient method uses a loop to output the message. Assuming that the message is defined by a DEFM pseudo operator at the end of the program, the program code performs as follows. The HL register pair is set to point to the first of the characters, the character is loaded into the accumulator and output to the display. The HL register pair is then incremented by one, so that it is pointing to the next character which is loaded into the accumulator and output to the display, and so on. Program 7.3 outputs a string of eleven characters to the display.

```
; Program 7.3 output text to the display
;
        LD   HL,TEXT    ; HL points to first character
        LD   B,11
;
NEXCH:  LD   A,(HL)     ; get next character
        CALL COUT
        INC  HL         ; HL points to next character
        DJNZ NEXCH
        HALT
;
TEXT:   DEFM 'ABCDEFGHIJK'
```

Exercise 7.5
Rewrite Program 7.3 so that instead of counting the number of characters to be output, characters are output until a byte containing zero is encountered.

The INC HL instruction in Program 7.3 is a new instruction for you to note. In fact all the register pairs, BC, DE, HL, SP, IX and IY, can be incremented by one with an INC rp instruction and also decremented by one with a DEC rp. One important difference between incrementing and decrementing register pairs and incrementing and decrementing single registers is that none of the flags is affected by the register pair INC and DEC instructions. Check this fact for yourself by looking at Table C.7 in Appendix C.

7.5   THE SUBROUTINE MECHANISM

Having used subroutines we are now going to see how they work, that is, what happens when a call is made from a main program to a subroutine and a return is made from that subroutine. The following description refers to Figure 7.3.

35

The stack is used by the subroutine mechanism to save temporarily the return address. When the main program CALL instruction is executed, the address of the instruction following the CALL instruction (NEXTI) is automatically pushed on to the stack. Execution of the subroutine is then started by loading the program counter (PC) register with the address specified in the CALL instruction (SUBR).

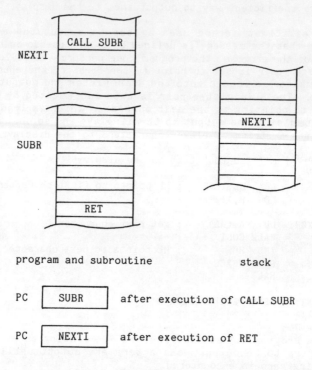

program and subroutine   stack

PC [SUBR]   after execution of CALL SUBR

PC [NEXTI]   after execution of RET

Figure 7.3

When the subroutine RET instruction is executed, the top of the stack (NEXTI) is automatically popped off into the PC register and the instruction at the address pointed to by the PC register (that is, the one following the CALL instruction - NEXTI) is executed next.

If a subroutine uses the stack for any reason, then it must ensure that it has popped off all that it has pushed on, so that when the RET instruction is executed the top of the stack contains the return address.

7.6 PROGRAM

Write a subroutine called CHSOUT which outputs a character n times on m lines on the display. On entry to the subroutine the accumulator contains the character and m and n are contained in the B and C registers, respectively.

Write a subroutine called TEXOUT which outputs a string of characters. On entry to the subroutine HL contains the address of the first character in the string. The string must be terminated by a byte containing a zero value.

Using the subroutines CHSOUT and TEXOUT and subroutines from previous programs, write a program which outputs the following on the display

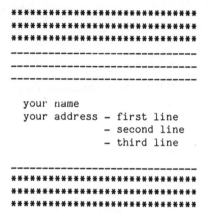

```
******************************
******************************
******************************
------------------------------
------------------------------
------------------------------

    your name
    your address - first line
                 - second line
                 - third line

------------------------------
******************************
******************************
******************************
```

As an extra challenge you could output after the last line the following pattern

```
******************************
 ************************** 
  ************************  
   **********************   
    ********************    
     ******************     
      ****************      
       **************       
        ************        
         **********         
          ********          
           ******           
            ****            
             **             
```

You should use nested loops to provide this additional output, not just fourteen calls to the TEXOUT subroutine with fourteen different fixed-character strings.

8   Carry and overflow

Carry and overflow are two conditions which can occur during addition and subtraction. The conditions affect bits in the flag register which can then be tested by conditional jump instructions.

8.1 CARRY

Carry normally refers to the carry out of the most significant bit during the addition of two numbers. For example, the sum

```
      00110011      (+51)
    + 00011100      (+28)
      --------
      01001111      (+79)
      --------
```

does not produce a carry, but the sum

```
      11111110      (-2)
    + 11111111      (-1)
      --------
  [1] 11111101      (-3)
      --------
```

has produced a carry which would be ignored as far as the result of the 8-bit addition is concerned.

Exercise 8.1
Does 11000000 + 01000000 produce a carry?

8.2 THE CARRY FLAG

When an ADD instruction is executed the CARRY FLAG will be set to 1 if carry occurs, otherwise it will be reset to 0. The carry flag can then be tested by using one of the conditional jump instructions

```
       JP    C,label
       JP    NC,label
       JR    C,label
   or  JR    NC,label
```

where C stands for Carry (the carry flag is set to 1) and NC stands for No Carry (the carry flag is reset to 0).

The carry flag is also used to indicate that a SUB instruction needed to borrow a 1 during subtraction of the two most significant bits.

Exercise 8.2
Will the instruction labelled NCARRY or CARRY be executed after the JP instruction in the following sequence?

```
        LD    A,7
        SUB   8
        JP    NC,NCARRY
CARRY:  -
```

The carry flag is involved in the execution of shift, rotate and decimal adjust instructions, which are dealt with later in the book.

There are two instructions which may be used to change the value of the carry flag. The instructions are SCF which Sets the Carry Flag to 1, and CCF which Complements the Carry Flag. These two instructions are specified in Table C.6 in Appendix C.

Exercise 8.3
Write a sequence of instructions which resets the carry flag to 0.

8.3 OVERFLOW

Overflow occurs when the result of an operation is outside an arithmetic range. For 8-bit registers and bytes the range is −128 to +127.

For addition, two numbers with different signs will never cause overflow. However, when adding two positive numbers or two negative numbers overflow may or may not occur. For example, the sum

```
      01100100        (+100)
    + 00110001        (+49)
      --------
      10010101        (-107)
      --------
```

does not produce the correct arithmetic result because the real sum of the two numbers, +149, is greater than +127 and is therefore outside the arithmetic range.

For subtraction, overflow can only occur if the two numbers have different signs. For example, the subtraction

```
      01111110        (+126)
    - 11000000        (-64)
      --------
 [1]  10111110        (-66)
      --------
```

39

does not produce the correct arithmetic result. The real result, +190, is outside the range. Additionally, in this particular example, carry has occurred.

Exercise 8.4
Carry can also occur with overflow when adding two numbers. Give an example of two 8-bit numbers which when added produce carry and overflow at the same time.

8.4 THE OVERFLOW FLAG

The parity/overflow flag is used to indicate overflow or parity depending on the instruction. The flag indicates overflow for arithmetic operations when it is referred to as the overflow flag.

The OVERFLOW FLAG is set to 1 if overflow occurs and reset to 0 if overflow does not occur, for the ADD, SUB, INC, DEC, NEG and CP instructions. The flag can be tested using one of the conditional jump instructions

```
      JP   PO,label
or    JP   PE,label
```

where PE stands for Overflow (the overflow flag is set to 1) and PO stands for No Overflow (the overflow flag is reset to 0). Unfortunately, PO and PE refer to the usage of the flag as a parity indicator and, therefore, are rather misleading when referring to overflow. Notice that there are no JR equivalent instructions for overflow.

8.5 CONDITIONAL CALLS AND RETS

In addition to the simple CALL subroutine instruction, there are conditional CALL instructions which operate in a similar manner to the conditional JP instructions. For example, the program segment

```
            JP   NZ,OVER
            CALL SUBEX
      OVER: -
```

could be recoded, using the single instruction

```
      CALL Z,SUBEX
```

thereby saving one instruction.

The conditions which can be tested by the conditional CALL instructions are the same as those which can be tested by the conditional JP instructions, that is, Z and NZ, M and P, C and NC and PE and PO.

There are equivalent conditional RET instructions to return

40

conditionally from a subroutine. However, these are not normally used because a subroutine should have only one exit place, that is, only one unconditional RET instruction.   Hence, the subroutine structure

```
            -
            JP   NC,EXIT
            -
            JP   EXIT
            -
            JP   Z,EXIT
            -
    EXIT:   RET
```

would be used in preference to

```
            -
            RET  NC
            -
            RET
            -
            RET  Z
            -
            RET
```

A single exit subroutine provides a cleaner interface which ensures that all that has to be done before returning is done and extensions to the subroutines can easily be made without the possibility of forgetting that exits were made other than at the end of the subroutine.

The 'exit' label is normally associated with the first of several instructions ending with the RET instruction. If, for example, registers have to be restored then the end of the subroutine may look like

```
            -
    GOBACK: POP  BC
            POP  DE
            RET
```

8.6 PROGRAM

Amend the subroutine NUMIN so that it inputs a signed, rather than unsigned, decimal number. The subroutine should then accept numbers such as −121, +84 and 53 (implied positive number).

Write a program which first requests two numbers to be input as follows

```
    INPUT FIRST NUMBER  n1
    INPUT SECOND NUMBER n2
```

and then outputs

```
    n1 + n2 IS znorp
```

41

where znorp is the word ZERO, NEGATIVE or POSITIVE, followed, if
appropriate, on the next line by

PRODUCED OVERFLOW

followed, if appropriate, on the next line by

PRODUCED CARRY

The two numbers n1 and n2 are signed 2-digit decimal numbers, for
example, 63 and -08.

The program should repeatedly deal with pairs of numbers until
END is input as n1.

9 Bit operations and the index registers

The Z80 has an extensive range of bit instructions. The bit instructions allow individual bits of a register or memory byte to be tested (for 0 or 1), set to 1 and reset to 0. The number of the bit in the register or memory byte to be used in the operation has to be specified in the instruction and, for this purpose, the bits are numbered right to left starting at 0, as follows

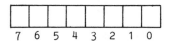

All bit instructions operate on any of one of the single registers or a memory byte pointed to by HL, IX or IY.

9.1 THE BIT TEST INSTRUCTION

The BIT instruction tests a specified bit of a register or memory byte and sets the zero flag accordingly - to 1 if the bit is 0, or to 0 if the bit is 1. For example, the instruction

        BIT 6,E

tests the bit numbered 6 of register E and would set the Z flag to 0 if register E contained 01000100B.

Look back at Program 3.2 where you will see a BIT instruction used to test bit 0 of the accumulator.

Exercise 9.1
What will be the value of the Z flag if a BIT 1,A instruction is executed when the accumulator contains FDH?

It is probably easier to remember that the BIT instruction causes the Z flag to be set to the complement of the specified bit.

A BIT instruction is usually followed by a 'jump on zero' or 'jump on non-zero' instruction, in which case the Zero and Non-Zero conditions refer, as you would expect, to the specified bit being 0 or 1, respectively. So there is normally no need to remember how the Z flag is set by a BIT instruction.

9.2   THE SET AND RES INSTRUCTIONS

The SET instruction allows a specified bit of a register or memory byte to be set to 1. For example, the instruction

        SET   2,C

sets bit 2 of register C to 1. The other bits of C remain unchanged.

The RES instruction allows a specified bit of a register or memory byte to be reset to 0. For example, the instruction

        RES   5,(HL)

resets bit 5 of the memory byte pointed to by HL to 0. The other bits of the memory byte remain unchanged.

Exercise 9.2
Write a program segment which checks if the number in the accumulator is odd or even and then sets bit 7 of the B register to 1 if the number is odd or to 0 if the number is even, without affecting the other bits in the B register.

9.3   THE DEFS PSEUDO OPERATOR

The DEFS pseudo operator allows memory bytes to be reserved, usually in the data area at the end of the program. Unlike the DEFB and the DEFM pseudo operators, the DEFS pseudo operator does not initialise the bytes to a specified value. For example, in the following program segment

```
            -
    NUM:    DEFS 1
    BUFFER: DEFS 96
    NAME:   DEFM 'FRED'
            -
```

the first DEFS pseudo operator reserves 1 byte which is labelled NUM, and the second DEFS reserves 96 bytes - the first of which is labelled BUFFER.

Exercise 9.,3
Referring to the program segment above, if the label NUM has a value of 100H what will be the value of the label NAME (in hexadecimal)?

Examples of the use of the DEFS pseudo operator appear in the remainder of this chapter.

9.4   THE INDEX REGISTERS

The Z80 microprocessor has two index registers, IX and IY, so-called because they allow a program to access a particular byte

44

in a block of bytes, by an index which is relative to the start of the block.

The following program skeleton shows how an index register can be used.

```
          LD    IX,START    ;IX points to start of block
          -
          LD    A,(IX+2)    ; A = 3rd byte of block
          -
          SET   3,(IX+5)    ; Bit 3 of 5th byte = 0
          -
          DEC   (IX+9)      ; Decrement last byte
          -
START:    DEFS 10
          -
```

A block of ten bytes is defined at the end of the program, using the DEFS pseudo operator. The first of the bytes is labelled START. Before any bytes in the block may be accessed the index register is set to point to this first byte using the LD IX,START instruction. Thereafter, a particular byte in the block is referenced by specifying the index register plus the relative displacement of the byte from the start of the block. For example, the fourth byte of the block is referenced by (IX+3).

Exercise 9.4
Referring to the program above, if the block of bytes were instead defined by START: DEFM 'ABCDEFGHIJ' what would the accumulator contain after execution of the instruction LD A,(IX+7)?

The IY index register can be used in exactly the same way as the IX index register.

The index registers are useful for referencing bytes within blocks in which the data is distinct but related; for example, in a structure in which a file or table contains records of data items.

However, in the main you will find the index registers being used with a zero displacement, in which case they are used in much the same way as the HL register pair.

9.5   EXPRESSIONS

Operands that we have used so far have consisted of a single label. In fact, the Z80 assembler allows a wide range of expressions to be written as an operand - a single label being the simplest example of an expression. For example, the instruction

```
          LD    A,(NUM+1)
```

would cause the contents of the byte following the byte labelled

NUM to be loaded into the accumulator.

When an expression is used it is normally a simple one, as in the LD instruction above. However, an expression may be quite complex as a result of using the many operators which can be used in an expression. The full list of the twenty available operators is shown in Appendix E.

All expressions are evaluated left to right, except that unary operators are performed first, exponentiation next, multiplication, division, modulo and shifts next, followed by addition and subtraction, and then logical operations and comparisons. 16-bit signed arithmetic is used throughout the evaluation of an expression.

The following program skeleton shows one use of expressions

```
ITEMS:  EQU  m
LENTH:  EQU  n
        -
        -
TABLE:  DEFS ITEMS*LENTH
```

The characteristics (number of items in the table and the number of bytes in each item) of the TABLE need to be varied from one version of the program to another. Thus the TABLE is defined in terms of its characteristics which are given values, m and n, at the beginning of the program (using the EQU pseudo operator) for a particular version of the program.

9.6   JUMP TABLES

A jump table is a convenient way of executing one of several program segments depending on the value of a variable which has sequential values 1 to n.

The basis of the technique is as follows

```
        -                       ; rp contains JPTAB + N - 1
        JP   (rp)
        -
JPTAB:  JP   N1CODE    ; start of jump table
        JP   N2CODE
        -
        JP   NNCODE    ; end of jump table
        -
```

Before the jump table can be used, one of the IX, IY or HL register pairs must contain the address of one of the JP instructions in the jump table. A JP (rp) instruction is then executed which causes one of the JP instructions in the jump table to be executed.

Program 9.1 shows the use of a jump table in displaying the name of a day whose number is input from the keyboard.

```
; Program 9.1 input day number, output day name
;
        CALL CINEKO     ; input day number
        SUB  30H
;
        LD   B,0        ; day number into BC
        LD   C,A
;
        LD   HL,DAYJP   ; HL contains start of jump table
        ADD  HL,BC      ;              + day number
        DEC  HL         ;              -1
;
        JP   (HL)
;
DAYJP:  JP   MON        ;jump table
        JP   TUE
        JP   WED
        JP   THU
        JP   FRI
        JP   SAT
        JP   SUN
;
MON:    LD   HL,MONDAY
        CALL TEXOUT
        JP   FINI
;
        —
        —

;
SUN:    LD   HL,SUNDAY
        CALL TEXOUT
        JP   FINI
;
FINI:   HALT
;
MONDAY: DEFM 'MONDAY'
        DEFB 0
        —
        —
SUNDAY: DEFM 'SUNDAY'
        DEFB 0
```

The day number, which is input from the keyboard, is in the range 1 to 7, representing the days Monday to Sunday. The address in the jump table of the corresponding JP instructions is calculated in the HL register pair, and execution of that JP instruction follows execution of the JP (HL) instruction. Hence, a jump is made to the program segment which outputs the name of the day corresponding to the number which was input.

Because the seven program segments are the same length (that is, they occupy the same number of bytes), an algorithm could have been used to compute the start address of the corresponding program segment, rather than using a jump table. However, the jump table technique makes the code more intelligible and, in fact, has to be used when the program segments are of unequal lengths.

9.7   PROGRAM

Write a program which inputs a number in the range 1 to 12 and outputs the corresponding name of the month.

Instead of using a 'jump table' technique to solve this problem, use a 'look-up table' technique as follows: set up two data areas at the end of your program, one in which the names of the months are stored end-on in a contiguous data area (occupying 74 bytes), and a second 12-byte data area in which the nth byte contains the position of the start of the nth month's name in the months' names data area (that is, the first of the 12 bytes will contain 0, the second 7, the third 15, and so on); to obtain the start address of a month's name, look-up the corresponding entry in the 12-byte data area and add it to the start address of the months' names data area.

10 Shift instructions, multiply and divide

Shift instructions allow the bits of a register or memory byte to be shifted one bit place to the left or to the right. There are two types of shift instructions - logical and arithmetic. Logical shifts consider the contents of the register or memory byte to be just a bit pattern when the shift is made. Arithmetic shifts consider the contents of the register or memory byte to be a signed number so that when the shift is made the number is arithmetically multiplied by two (left shift) or divided by two (right shift). The Z80 microprocessor has one logical instruction and two arithmetic instructions. Descriptions of the shift instructions are included in Table C.8 in Appendix C.

10.1 THE SRL INSTRUCTION

The Shift Right Logical instruction shifts a register or memory byte one bit place to the right. Bit 7 of the register or memory byte is reset to 0 and the original bit 0 goes into the carry flag, as follows

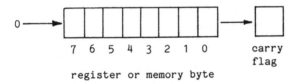

```
7 6 5 4 3 2 1 0          carry
                         flag
   register or memory byte
```

The form of the instruction is

      SRL   m

where m is any of the single registers or a memory byte pointed to by HL, IX or IY.

Exercise 10.1
Assuming that the contents of the accumulator and carry flag are A7H and 0, respectively, what will be their contents after the execution of an SRL A instruction?

In all shift instructions, the bit which is moved out of the register or memory byte, be it to the left or right, is placed in the carry flag. This can be useful because the value of a bit which has been moved out can be checked by any of the carry conditional jumps, such as JP C,label and JR NC,label.

10.2   THE SRA INSTRUCTION

The Shift Right Arithmetic instruction is the same as the SRL instruction except that, instead of bit 7 being reset to 0 it is set to what it was before the shift. In other words, the sign bit remains unchanged so that a positive value would remain positive and a negative value would remain negative. The SRA instruction, in fact, divides the register or memory byte by two, and leaves the remainder in the carry flag.

The form of the instruction is

        SRA   m

where m is any of the single registers or a memory byte pointed to by HL, IX or IY.

Exercise 10.2
Give the contents of the B register, the C register and the carry flag, in binary and decimal, after the execution of each of the instructions in the following program segment

        LD   B,11
        SRA   B
        LD   C,-8
        SRA   C

10.3   THE SLA INSTRUCTION

The Shift Left Arithmetic instruction shifts a register or memory byte one bit place to the left. In doing so, bit 0 of the register or memory byte is reset to 0 and bit 7 is placed in the carry flag, as follows

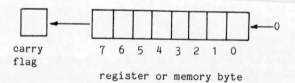

carry
flag   7 6 5 4 3 2 1 0

register or memory byte

The effect of the instruction is to multiply the contents of the register or memory byte by two.

The usual difference between an arithmetic left shift and a logical left shift is that the overflow flag would be set accordinglyfor an arithmetic left shift but not for a logical left shift. Overflow would occur, for example, during an arithmetic left shift when the register contained 127 since, in signed number arithmetic, multiplying 127 by 2 would cause overflow in an 8-bit register.

As the shift left arithmetic instruction does not set the overflow flag, it should more precisely be called a shift left logical instruction.

If the contents of the register or memory byte to be shifted left are considered to be an unsigned number in the range 0 to 255, then the carry flag would indicate overflow.

The form of the instruction is

    SLA m

where m is any one of the single registers, or a memory byte pointed to by HL, IX or IY.

Exercise 10.3
Using the SLA and ADD instructions write a program segment which multiplies the contents of the accumulator by ten, using the fact that 10 x N is equivalent to 2 x N + 2 x 2 x 2 x N.

10.4   8-BIT MULTIPLICATION AND DIVISION

The multiplication method of repeated addition which we have been using is very inefficient for multipliers greater than five, or so. A more efficient method for larger multipliers is called 'shift and add'. To understand the reason for using this method work through the following multiplication

```
          00111        multiplicand
     x    01010        multiplier
          -----
          00000        x 0
          00111        x 10
         00000         x 000
         00111         x 1000
        00000          x 00000
       ----------
       001000110       product
       ----------
```

Each bit in the multiplier causes a one bit shift to the left of the multiplicand which is then added into the product. Also, it can be seen that the value to be added in each time is either the multiplicand or zero.

Hence, the algorithm for multiplication by 'shift and add' is: for each bit of the multiplier, working from right to left, the multiplicand is added to the partial product if the multiplier bit is 1, otherwise nothing is done: The multiplicand is then shifted left one bit place before the next bit of the multiplier is considered.

Program 10.1 shows a program segment which multiplies the
contents of the B and C registers, using the 'shift and add'
method. The product is accumulated in the accumulator.

```
        ; Program 10.1 computes A = B x C
        ;
                -
                LD   A,0
                LD   D,7
        NEXBIT: SRL  C            ; test next bit of multiplier
                JP   NC,NOADD
                ADD  A,B          ; add in multiplicand
                JR   PO,OVERFL
        NOADD:  DEC  D
                JR   Z,DONE
                SLA  B            ; shift multiplicand
                JR   NEXBIT
                -
```

The program segment deals only with positive signed numbers. It
would have to be extended to deal with negative signed numbers.
One straightforward method of doing this is first to multiply the
absolute values of the two numbers and then compute the sign of
the product according to the signs of the numbers.

The operation of Program 10.1 is as follows: the next multiplier
bit is tested for 0 or 1 by shifting the bit into the carry flag;
using a carry flag conditional jump instruction the multiplicand
is added in, or not; the multiplicand is then shifted left one
bit place ready to be added in, or not, when the next multiplier
bit is tested. A check for an overflow condition is made when
the multiplicand is added in.

Division can be performed by 'repeated subtraction' (equivalent
to multiplication by 'repeated addition') or by a method which is
similar to the standard pencil and paper approach, in which a
check is made to see if the divisor goes into the remaining
dividend (equivalent, in some respects, to multiplication by
'shift and add' and could, in fact, be referred to as the 'shift
and subtract' technique).

10.5   PROGRAM

Write a new MULT subroutine which uses the 'shift and add' method
of multiplication and additionally deals with signed numbers.

Write a subroutine called DIV which divides a signed number in
register B by a signed number in register C and leaves the
quotient in the accumulator and the remainder in register D.

Using the DIV subroutine to divide by ten, write a subroutine
called NUMOUT which outputs the contents of the accumulator as a
signed number in the range -128 to +127. Leading zeros should
not be output and positive numbers should be output without a +
character.

Using the NUMOUT, DIV and MULT subroutines and subroutines from previous programs, write a main program which inputs two signed numbers separated by either an * character or a / character and followed by an = character. The program should then output either the product of the number (if the * character was input), or the quotient and remainder (if the / character was input). A typical dialogue would look like

    -11*55=-55
    125/10=12 REMAINDER 5

11 Logical operations and macros

11.1 LOGIC OPERATORS

There are several Z80 logical instructions which allow logical operations to be performed between corresponding bits in the accumulator and an 8-bit operand.

To understand the operation of the logical instructions, it is necessary to know the rules of the basic logical operators, such as AND, OR, XOR (Exclusive OR) and NOT. The rules are normally displayed in tables as follows

```
0 AND 0 = 0        0 OR 0 = 0        0 XOR 0 = 0        NOT 0 = 1
0 AND 1 = 0        0 OR 1 = 1        0 XOR 1 = 1        NOT 1 = 0
1 AND 0 = 0        1 OR 0 = 1        1 XOR 0 = 1
1 AND 1 = 1        1 OR 1 = 1        1 XOR 1 = 0
```

Apart from the NOT operator, logical operators operate on two one-bit values and produce a one-bit result. For example, the result of the AND operator is one if, and only if, the two values are one, otherwise, the result is zero.

Glance at Table C.5 in Appendix C where you will see the AND, OR and XOR instructions specified. Notice that the Symbolic Operation column of that table uses the Boolean Algebra symbols of ^ for AND, v for OR and ⊕ for XOR.

Exercise 11.1
Express the operation of the XOR logical operator in words.

11.2 LOGICAL INSTRUCTIONS

All the Z80 logical instructions perform a logical operation between the bits in the accumulator and their corresponding bits in the operand, leaving the result in the accumulator. For example, if the accumulator contains 00001010B and register B contains 11001111B then the instruction AND B would produce a result of 00001010B in the accumulator, as follows

```
    Contents of A                      00001010B
    Contents of B                      11001111B
    Contents of A after AND B          00001010B
```

Corresponding bits in the accumulator and operand are logically operated upon in isolation from the other bits.

The operand of a logical instruction may be a register, an 8-bit value or a memory byte pointed to by HL, IX or IY. The logical instructions may be specified together as

$$
\left.\begin{matrix} \text{AND} \\[8pt] \text{OR} \\[8pt] \text{XOR} \end{matrix}\right\} \quad \left\{\begin{matrix} r \\ n \\ \text{(HL)} \\ \text{(IX)} \\ \text{(IY)} \end{matrix}\right.
$$

Notice that the accumulator is implied in the instructions since logical operations may be performed only on the accumulator.

The NOT logical operation is performed by the CPL instruction which changes all the 0's in the accumulator to 1's and all the 1's to 0's. The mnemonic CPL stands for the word 'ComPLement'.

Exercise 11.2
Give the contents of the accumulator and the S, Z and C flags, in binary, after the execution of each instruction of the following sequence

```
LD    A,10110101B
LD    C,11110000B
AND   00011111B
OR    C
XOR   11001100B
CPL
```

11.3   MASKING

One of the main uses of the AND logical instruction is in masking when it is required to use only some of the bits of an 8-bit value and it is necessary to mask the required bits. For example, masking could be used instead of subtraction to obtain a decimal digit's value from its character code, because the least significant four bits of a decimal digit's character code are its value and can be obtained by ANDing the character code with 00001111B, as follows

```
LD    A,'7'    ; accumulator containing 00110111B
AND   OFH      ;            ANDed with  00001111B
               ; gives a value of        00000111B
```

Exercise 11.3
Write a logical instruction which will convert a decimal digit value in the accumulator to its character code.

11.4   MACROS

Macros provide a means for a programmer to define his own opcodes. Suppose that there is a frequent need to reset the

carry flag to 0 in a program, then an opcode to do that could be
defined at the beginning of the program with the following macro
definition

```
RSF:    MACRO           ; reset carry flag macro
        SCF             ; * macro body
        CCF             ; *
        ENDM            ; end of macro definition
```

The macro pseudo operator informs the assembler that a macro
called RSF is to be defined. The code between MACRO and ENDM
(the macro-end pseudo operator) is called the macro body.

Now, at any place in the program the opcode RSF can be used - or,
as is usually said, 'the macro RSF can be called'. For example,
the RSF macro is called in the following program segment

```
        LD    (POINT),A
        RSF               ; reset carry flag macro
        ADD   A,B
```

During assembly the program segment will be expanded, according
to the macro definition, to

```
        LD    (POINT),A
        SCF               ; macro RSF
        CCF               ; expansion
        ADD   A,B
```

Exercise 11.4
Write a macro which multiplies the contents of the accumulator by
four and give an example of a call to the macro.

A growing use of macros is in the attempt to give assembly
language programs some structure (similar to the structuring
facilities of high-level languages) for constructs which are
often used. Program 11.1 shows how macros can be used to give
some structuring to loops.

Two macros are defined - one for the start of the loop, LOOPST,
and one for the end of the loop, LOOPEN. Unlike the previous RSF
macro, both of these macros have parameters. Any parameters used
in a macro definition must be listed after the MACRO pseudo
operator. The parameters may then by used anywhere in the macro
body. When a call is made to a macro with parameters, during
expansion of the macro the parameters are replaced by the actual
parameters in the macro call. The last macro call in Program
11.1 would be expanded to

```
        DEC   E
        JP    NZ,ROUND
```

Notice that parameters in a macro definition are preceded by the
character and parameters in a macro call are enclosed with
apostrophes.

```
; Program 11.1 structured loops using macros
;
LOOPST: MACRO #R,#N          ; start of loop macro
        LD     #R,#N
        ENDM
;
LOOPEN: MACRO #R,#LABEL       ; end of loop macro
        DEC    #R
        JP     NZ,#LABEL
        ENDM
;
        -
        LOOPST 'C','99'
NEXTHG: -
        -
        LOOPEN 'C','NEXTHG'
        -
        LOOPST 'E','18'
ROUND:  -
        -
        LOOPEN 'E','ROUND'
        -
```

Macro definitions may not be nested, but a previously defined
macro may be called from another macro body.

In order to be able to use labels which are local to a macro body
a special symbol generator facility is provided. This facility
is best explained by way of an example. Consider the macro
definition

```
TIMER:   MACRO #N
         LD    B,#N
TM#$YM:  DJNZ  TM#$YM
         ENDM
```

which provides a crude timing facility by counting down register
B from N to zero. A local label is required for the loop, but if
this label were to be chosen in the normal way as, say TMLOOP,
then a program which called the TIMER macro more than once would
cause multiple definitions of the TMLOOP label to be produced
during macro expansion of the program. To overcome this problem,
local labels are defined with the last four characters as #$YM
and during the expansion of macros, #$YM is replaced by a 4-digit
hexadecimal number starting at 0000 for the first macro call and
incrementing by one for each subsequent macro call.

For example, a program containing three calls on the TIMER
macro, as follows

```
              -
        TIMER '200'
              -
        TIMER '50'
              -
        TIMER '76'
              -
```

would be expanded as

```
              -
        LD    B,200
TM0000: DJNZ  TM0000
              -
        LD    B,50
TM0001: DJNZ  TM0001
              -
        LD    B,76
TM0002: DJNZ  TM0002
              -
```

The main difference between macros and subroutines is that
instructions in a macro body are repeated everywhere that a macro
is called, whereas subroutine instructions occur once only.   In
general, macros should not be used when the macro body consists
of more than just a few instructions.

The format for defining and calling macros does, unfortunately,
vary from one Z80 assembly language system to another. You should
obtain the correct format for your system from the macro section
in your Z80 assembly language manual.

11.5   CONDITIONAL PSEUDO OPERATIONS

Conditional pseudo operations provide the capability to include
conditionally parts of a program during assembly time.   The two
conditional pseudo operators are COND and ENDC, and they are used
as follows

```
              -
        COND    CODEIN
              -
              -
        ENDC
              -
```

The instructions between the COND and ENDC pseudo operators will
be included during assembly if the value of CODEIN is non-zero,
but ignored by the assembler if CODEIN is zero.

The DEFL - DEFine Label - pseudo operator is normally used to set
the value of the COND pseudo operator label to zero or non-zero.
For example, if the statement

had appeared before the COND pseudo operator, in the above
example, the instruction between the COND and ENDC pseudo
operators would be included in the assembly.

Although the condition usually depends on the value of a label,
an arithmetic or logical expression may be used.

Exercise 11.5
A program can be assembled to produce output to a display or a
printer. The program has two subroutines, with the same name –
one subroutine for outputting to the display, the other for
outputting to the printer. Using the conditional and DEFL pseudo
operators sketch out the relevant parts of the program to show
how it can be assembled for either display output or printer
output.

The DEFL pseudo operator is similar to the EQU pseudo operator.
Both operators allow a label to be given a value but, whereas the
EQU pseudo operator can appear only once for any label in a
program, the DEFL pseudo operator can be repeated in the same
program to give different values to a label. This extra facility
of the DEFL pseudo operator allows more flexible conditional
assemblies to be constructed.

The conditional pseudo operations are very useful for tailoring a
general program for a particular requirement.

11.6   PROGRAM

Two other common logical operations are NOR and NAND, which are
short for NOT OR and NOT AND, respectively. The rules of these
two logical operations are

0 NOR 0 = 1	0 NAND 0 = 1
0 NOR 1 = 0	0 NAND 1 = 1
1 NOR 0 = 0	1 NAND 0 = 1
1 NOR 1 = 0	1 NAND 1 = 0

from which it can be seen that the result of the NOR operation is
the complement, or NOT, of the OR result and, similarly, the
result of the NAND operation is the NOT of the AND result.

Write a Logic Operation Trainer program which repeatedly allows
input of the form

    b lop b = b

where b is 0 or 1
and   lop is one of OR   (space to be input after the R)
                     AND
                     XOR
                     NOR
          or   NAN (short for NAND)

and outputs further along the same line, TRUE if the input is correct and otherwise FALSE.

You may assume that the input is valid. A training session is ended by inputting the letter E.

12   Rotate instructions and parity

Rotate instructions are similar to shift instructions except that the bit shifted out of one end is shifted into the other end - hence, the name rotate.

There are several rotate instructions available in the Z80 microprocessor. Four of the rotate instructions involve the accumulator; the other rotate instructions involve a register or memory byte.

Some of the rotate instructions include the carry flag within the rotation, while others, referred to as rotate circular instructions, do not.

In line with the shift instructions, rotates may be left or right and are for one bit place only. All rotates are a logical type of shift.

The definition of all the rotate instructions is included in Table C.8 in Appendix C.

12.1   ACCUMULATOR ROTATE INSTRUCTIONS

The accumulator can be rotated left and right, and for each direction the carry flag may, or may not, be included within the rotate, giving the four instructions

	RLA	- rotate left accumulator,
	RRA	- rotate right acccumulator,
	RLCA	- rotate left circular accumulator,
and	RRCA	- rotate right circular accumulator.

The Rotate Left Accumulator instruction includes the carry flag within the rotate and operates as follows

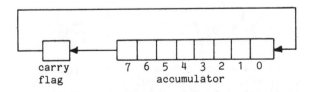

carry flag   7 6 5 4 3 2 1 0   accumulator

The contents of the accumulator move to the left one bit place, and in doing so, bit 7 of the accumulator moves into the carry flag and the carry flag moves round into bit 0 of the accumulator.

The Rotate Right Accumulator instruction also includes the carry flag within the rotate and operates as follows

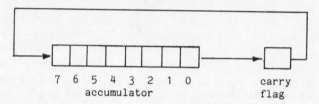

7 6 5 4 3 2 1 0
accumulator

carry
flag

The contents of the accumulator move to the right one bit place, and in doing so, bit 0 of the accumulator moves into the carry flag and the carry flag moves round into bit 7 of the accumulator.

The Rotate Left Circular Accumulator instruction is a circular version of a rotate and does not, therefore, include the carry flag within the rotate. However, the carry flag is still involved as follows

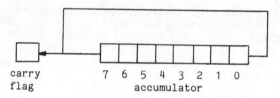

carry
flag

7 6 5 4 3 2 1 0
accumulator

The contents of the accumulator move to the left one bit place, and in doing so, bit 7 of the accumulator is moved to the carry flag and around into bit 0 of the accumulator. So after a RLCA instruction the carry flag and bit 0 of the accumulator will always be the same value – the value of bit 7 of the accumulator prior to execution of the instruction.

The Rotate Right Circular Accumulator instruction is also a circular type of rotate and operates as follows

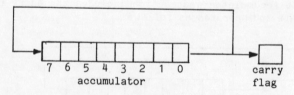

7 6 5 4 3 2 1 0
accumulator

carry
flag

The contents of the accumulator move to the right one bit place, andin doing so, bit 0 of the accumulator is moved into the carry flag and also around into bit 7 of the accumulator.

Exercise 12.1
Assuming that the accumulator contains 10101011B and the carry
flag contains 0, what will be the contents of the accumulator and
carry flag, in binary, after execution of each of the
instructions in the following sequence?

          RLA
          RLCA
          RRA
          RRCA

12.2   REGISTER AND MEMORY BYTE ROTATE INSTRUCTIONS

The four types of rotate of the accumulator may be applied to any
of the single registers or a memory byte, using the four
instructions

       RL m — rotate left register or memory byte,
       RR m = rotate right register or memory byte,
       RLC m — rotate left circular register or memory byte,
and   RRC m — rotate right circular register or memory byte,

where m is any one of the single registers or a memory byte
pointed to by HL, IX or IY.

The operation of the instructions is exactly the same as their
corresponding accumulator rotate instructions.

Exercise 12.2
Using the Table C.8 in Appendix C detect the differences between
the number of bytes occupied by, and the flag setting of the two
groups of instructions

       RLCA   and   RLC
       RLA   RL
       RRCA   RRC
       RRA   RR

Because a rotate accumulator instruction occupies only one byte
where as a shift accumulator occupies two bytes, some programmers
use the rotate accumulator instruction to perform a shift
operation, instead of the shift accumulator instruction.
However, in saving a byte, and time of execution of the
instruction, the program becomes less intelligible because what
is actually a shift operation appears in the program as a rotate
operation.

12.3   PACKING AND UNPACKING

The term packing refers to having a register or memory byte
containing two or more distinct values. We say that the values
are packed into the register or memory byte. For example, a
memory byte could be packed with the sex and age of a person, as
follows

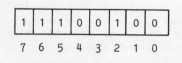

1	1	1	0	0	1	0	0

```
7   6   5   4   3   2   1   0
```

```
sex            age
```

Bit 7 of the memory byte indicates the sex of the person, say 0 for female and 1 for male. Bits 6 to 0 of the memory byte contain the person's age, giving a range for the age of 0 to 127. The example above specifies a male aged 100 years.

Assuming that the sex and age of one thousand people was held in memory then there is a saving of one thousand bytes by including the sex bit in the byte containing the age. If the sex and age were contained in separate bytes, two thousand bytes would be needed to hold the same information.

To be able to use the packed values it is usually necessary to unpack them. For example, to use the sex and age as packed above it would be necessary to unpack the sex bit into one register and the age bits into another register.

In general, packing is performed by ORing and shifting or rotating, while unpacking is performed by ANDing and shifting or rotating. For example, the program segment

```
        LD    A,(SEXAGE)
        AND   10000000B
        RLCA
        LD    B,A
        LD    A,(SEXAGE)
        AND   01111111B
        LD    C,A
```

unpacks a sex/age memory byte by placing the sex in the B register and the age in the C register. There are many ways of unpacking bytes, some using fewer instructions than others, and some more obvious than others. The method of unpacking also depends on the number, length and position of values that are packed.

Exercise 12.3
Write a program segment which packs into a memory byte labelled SEXAGE, sex from the B register (bit 0) and age from the C register.

12.4   PARITY

Parity refers to the number of 1's in a binary number. A binary number is said to have even parity if the number of 1's is even, and odd parity if the number of 1's is odd. For example,

```
           01101000   has odd parity,
           11111100   has even parity,
  and      01110011   has odd parity.
```

Parity is often used in computer systems when transferring
information from one unit to another. A parity bit is added to
the information at source to make the number of 1 bits either odd
or even. At the destination, the parity of the information is
checked to make sure that it is still either odd or even. It is
not a foolproof check because the parity would remain correct if
an even number of bits changed their values during transfer.
However, a parity check is a great deal better than nothing.

Exercise 12.4
Assuming an even parity system with bit 7 of a byte as the parity
bit, what will be the hexadecimal value of a byte containing the
ASCII character code for (i) X, and for (ii) +, with the parity
bit correctly set?

12.5   THE PARITY FLAG

The parity/overflow flag is used to indicate the parity of a
result after most of the rotate instructions and the shift and
logical instructions.

If the number of 1's in the register or memory byte is even after
any of these instructions has executed, the parity flag will be
set to 1, but if the number of 1's is odd the parity flag will be
reset to 0.

Exercise 12.5
Assuming that the accumulator contains B9H, what will be the
value of the parity flag after each of the instructions in the
following program segment?

```
          AND    OFEH
          SLA    A
          RLA
```

The parity condition can be tested by any of the instructions

```
          JP    PE,label
          JP    PO,label
          CALL PE,label
          CALL PO,label
          RET  PE
  and     RET  PO
```

The mnemonics PE and PO stand for Parity Even and Parity Odd,
respectively.

Exercise 12.6
Write a subroutine called CHKPAR which checks the parity of the
accumulator. On entry to the subroutine register B contains
either 0 to indicate an even parity check, or 1 to indicate an

odd parity check. On exit from the subroutine the register C
should contain 0 if the parity was correct and 1 otherwise.

12.6   PROGRAM

Write a subroutine called BINOUT which outputs on the display the
contents of the accumulator as eight binary digits.   The
subroutine will have to extract each bit separately from the
accumulator and output the character code for 1 or 0 depending on
the value of a bit.

Write a subroutine called PACK which packs the accumulator from
four consecutive memory bytes as follows

        bits 1 to 0 of M   to bits 7 to 6 of the accumulator,
        bits 1 to 0 of M+1   to bits 5 to 4 of the accumulator,
        bit 0   of M+2   to bit 3 of the accumulator,
    and bits 2 to 0 of M+3   to bits 2 to 0 of the accumulator,

where M is the first memory byte.

The address of the first of the four bytes is contained in the HL
register pair on entry to the subroutine.

Write a subroutine called UNPACK which does the reverse of the
PACK subroutine.

Using the subroutines BINOUT, PACK and UNPACK and existing
subroutines, write a main program which inputs ten sets of four
numbers and packs each set as specified in the PACK subroutine
specification. The four numbers are input as decimal numbers 0
to 3, 0 to 3, 0 to 1 and 0 to 7, respectively. The ten sets of
packed numbers should be stored in ten consecutive bytes. After
inputting the ten sets of numbers, the program should output each
of the packed sets in binary for checking purposes.

13   16-bit and multiple byte arithmetic

So far we have been concerned with 8-bit arithmetic - that is, 8-bit operands and 8-bit results. The range of numeric values which can be manipulated by 8-bit arithmetics is small and so we may need to use 16-bit arithmetic and more. The Z80 microprocessor has instructions which allows 16-bit arithmetic to be performed directly. These instructions can also be used to provide 32-bit arithmetic, 48-bit arithmetic and so on. The 16-bit arithmetic instructions also allow additional loop facilities.

All the 16-bit arithmetic instructions are described in Table C.7 in Appendix C.

13.1   THE DEFW PSEUDO OPERATOR

When working with 8-bit quantities we used the DEFB pseudo operator when it was necessary to initialise memory bytes at the end of our programs. When working with 16-bit quantities we will need to initialise double bytes, or words as they are called. To do this we use the DEFW (DEFine Word) pseudo operator. For example,

        DOUBLE: DEFW 56ABH

initialises DOUBLE to the value 56ABH. The label DOUBLE is associated with the first of the two bytes and, in fact, ABH is placed in the first of the two bytes and 56H in the second byte. This unusual ordering is necessary to complement the instructions which load register pairs with two consecutive bytes. For example, the instruction LD HL,(LABEL) loads register L with the first memory byte (LABEL) and register H with the second memory byte (LABEL+1).

In fact, the DEFW pseudo operation saves us having to concern ourselves with this reverse ordering. The LD HL,(LABEL) instruction in

        LD   HL,(LABEL)
        -
    LABEL: DEFW 7B9AH

will cause HL to be loaded with 7B9AH as you would expect.

13.2   THE 16-BIT ADD, ADC and SBC instructions

The main 16-bit arithmetic instructions use the HL register pair
as the 'accumulator'. For example, the 16-bit addition
instruction

        ADD   HL,DE

adds the contents of register pair DE to HL, leaving the result
in HL. The general form of the instruction is

        ADD   HL,ss

where ss is any one of the register pairs BC, DE, HL or SP.

The program segment

        LD   BC,2054
        LD   HL,1362
        ADD   HL,BC

shows two 16-bit numbers being added together in the HL register
pair. After execution of the ADD HL,BC instruction HL will
contain the value 3416.

Exercise 13.1
What is the range, in decimal, of signed numbers which can be
dealt with by 16-bit arithmetic?

Another 16-bit add instruction adds the carry produced by a
previous operation. The general form of the 16-bit ADd with
Carry instruction is

        ADC   HL,ss

where ss is the same as for the 16-bit ADD instruction. The
contents of the register pair ss are added to HL along with the
carry flag and the result is placed in HL.

The ADC HL,ss instruction can be used to provide a simple 32-bit
arithmetic facility. Look at Program 13.1 which shows a program
segment which adds two 32-bit signed numbers.

First, the least significant 16 bits of the two 32-bit numbers
are added using the ADD HL,DE instruction, and stored in the
result bytes. During this addition any carry out of the addition
of the most significant bit will be recorded in the carry flag.

Second, the most significant 16 bits of the numbers are added
using the ADC HL,DE instruction, which will cause the carry flag
to be added also - that is, the carry from the addition of the
least significant 16 bits of the numbers.

```
; Program 13.1   addition of two 32-bit signed numbers
;
          LD    HL,(N1LS)
          LD    DE,(N2LS)
          ADD   HL,DE          ; add least significant 16-bits
          LD    (RESLS),HL
          LD    HL,(N1MS)
          LD    DE,(N2MS)
          ADC   HL,DE          ; add most significant 16-bits
          LD    (RESMS),HL
          JP    PO,OVERF       ; overflow occurred?
N1MS:     DEFW  05A1H          ; first number
N1LS:     DEFW  63B2H
N2MS:     DEFW  00C6H          ; second number
N2LS:     DEFW  0A57EH
RESMS:    DEFW  0              ; result
RESLS:    DEFW  0
```

Hence, the overall affect of the program segment is to add two
32-bit signed numbers. Overflow is detected by checking the
overflow flag after execution of the ADC instruction.

Exercise 13.2
Referring to Program 13.1, what will be the contents of RESMS and
RESLS, in hexadecimal, at the end of execution of the program
segment?

The above technique can be extended to add multiple 16-bit
numbers.

There is only one 16-bit subtract instruction - a 'subtract with
carry' version. The general form of the 16-bit SuBtract with
Carry is

      SBC HL,ss

where ss is any one of the register pairs BC, DE, HL and SP - the
same as for the 16-bit add instructions.

The instruction causes the contents of the register pair ss and
the carry flag both to be subtracted from HL, the result being
left in the HL register pair.

The SBC HL,ss instruction can be used, in a similar way to the
ADC HL,ss instruction, to perform subtractions with multiple 16-
bit numbers.

To perform subtraction with single 16-bit numbers, it is
necessary to set the carry flag to 0 just prior to execution of
the SBC HL,ss instruction to ensure that nothing other than zero
is subtracted from the true result.

Exercise 13.3
Write a program segment which subtracts the contents of the
register pair BC from HL, assuming single 16-bit arithmetic.

One important point to note about the 16-bit ADD, ADC and SBC
instructions is the flag setting of these instructions. Look at
the specifications of these instructions in Table C.7 of Appendix
C and you will see that the 16-bit ADC and SBC instructions set
the carry, zero, overflow and sign flags as you woulld expect,
but the 16-bit ADD instruction causes only the carry flag to be
set. A 16-bit ADC instruction, preceded by an instruction to set
the carry flag to zero, can be used if the setting of the zero,
overflow and sign flags are required during a single 16-bit
addition.

13.3   EXTENDED LOOPS

The 16-bit load, increment/decrement and arithmetic instructions
which we have already considered can be used for loops in which
the loop index has a range of 0 to 65535. However, there are
special 16-bit instructions involving the IX and IY index
register pairs which can be used for such loops.

The basic loop structure using the IX index register looks like

```
        LD   IX,nn      ; or LD IX,(nn)
LOOP:   -
        -               ; instructions to be repeated
        -
        INC  IX         ; or DEC  IX
        JP   LOOP
```

The IX index register pair is first loaded with an initial value,
either directly using an LD IX,nn instruction, or indirectly
using an LD IX,(LABEL) instruction. At the end of the set of
instructions to be repeated, the index register is incremented by
one using an INC IX instruction, or decremented by one using a
DEC IX instruction. A jump is then made back to the first of the
instructions to be repeated.

The loop must be terminated either by a condition occurring
within the loop or by IX becoming a specific value. However, it
must be remembered that the INC IX and DEC IX instructions do not
affect any of the flags.

The IY index register can be used wherever the IX index register
can be used.

There is a special ADD instruction relating to the index
registers which, amongst other things, allows the registers to be
incremented and decremented by a value other than one, when used
as the loop index register. The instructions are

        ADD IX,pp

where pp is any one of the register pairs BC, DE, IX and SP and

        ADD   IY,rr

where rr is any one of the register pairs BC, DE, IY and SP. The instructions cause the contents of the register pair pp and rr to be added to IX and IY, respectively.

The use of the ADD IY,rr instruction is shown in Program 13 which outputs the numbers 1000 to 0 in decrements of 5.

```
        ; Program 13.2  outputs numbers 1000, 995, 990, ... 5, 0
        ;
                LD    DE,-5      ; DE contains decrement
                LD    IY,1000    ; IY contains first number
        ;
NEXNUM: CALL IYOUT
        CALL CRLF

        ADD   IY,DE      ; decrement IY
                         ; check if IY is 0
        PUSH IY          ; move IY to BC
        POP   BC
        LD    A,B
        CP    0          ; B zero?
        JP    NZ,NEXNUM  ; no
        LD    A,C
        CP    0          ; C zero?
        JP    N2,NEXNUM  ; no
        HALT
```

The index register IY which is used as the loop index is initialised to the first number,1000, and the register pair is set to the decrement (negative increment) value.

Each time through the loop a carriage-return line-feed is output to the display followed by the value in IY - the IYOUT subroutine outputs the contents of the IY register as an unsigned number in the range 0 to 65535.

After the repeated instructions IY is decremented by 5, that is, DE, containing -5, is added to IY. It is then necessary to check if IY is zero. This check is not as straightforward as you might think.   There are several methods of performing the check; none of them is a neat method. In Program 13.2 the check is made by splitting IY into the two registers B and C each of which is then checked for zero.

You will often find that the IX and IY index registers are awkward to use and that the other register pairs, particularly HL, are more convenient to use because there is a wider range of more flexible instructions involving these register pairs.

13.4   MULTIPLE BYTE ARITHMETIC

There are two instructions which can be used for multiple byte
arithmetic, in the same way that we saw that the two ADC HL, ss
and SBC HL,s instructions could be used for multiple 16-bit
arithmetic.

The equivalent add instruction is

    ADC   A,s

where s is either a value, a single register or a memory byte
pointed to by HL, IX or IY. The instruction causes s to be added
to the accumulator along with the carry flag.

The equivalent subtract instruction is

    SBC   A,s

where s is the same as for the ADC A,s instruction.   This
instruction causes s and the carry flag to be subtracted from the
accumulator.

The principle of multibyte arithmetic is that the two least
significant bytes of the numbers to be added (subtracted) are
added (subtracted) using an ADD (SUB) instruction and the
remaining pairs of bytes, going from the next least significant
byte to the most significant byte, are added (subtracted) using
the ADC (SBC) instruction.

Depending on the number of bytes to be added, there are many
combinations of 8-bit arithmetic instructions and 16-bit
arithmetic instructions which can be used. However, for the
general case of any number of bytes (which may, therefore, be an
odd number), an appropriate number of 8-bit arithmetic
instructions is most suitable.

Program 13.3 shows a program segment which adds multiple byte
numbers.

```
        ; Program 13.3 addition of multiple byte numbers
        ;
                -
                SCF             ; reset carry flag
                CCF
        ;
        NEXBYT: LD    A,(IX)
                ADC   A,(IY)    ; add next pair of bytes
                LD    (HL),A    ; and store result
                DEC   IX
                DEC   IY        ; point to next more significant
                                  bytes
                DEC   HL
                DJNZ NEXBYT
                -               ; addition done
```

72

Initially, the registers IX, IY and HL point to the least significant bytes of the first number, the second number and the sum, respectively, and the B register contains the number of bytes to be added. The carry flag must be initialised to 0 before the loop is entered so that the first add instruction is equivalent to an ADD instruction.

Exercise 13.4
What modifications need to be made to the program segment in Program 13.3 to make it subtract the second number from the first number?

13.5 PROGRAM

Write a program which outputs on the display, one per line, the numbers from m to n in steps of k.

The numbers m, n and k are unsigned hexadecimal numbers which the program inputs from the keyboard.

The level of difficulty of this program may be varied by restricting the values of m, n and k to fit into

     8-bits (8-bit arithmetic),
     16 bits (16-bit arithmetic or double 8-bit arithmetic),
     24 bits (16-bit arithmetic for the least significant 16
              bits and 8-bit arithmetic for the most
              significant 8 bits),
     32 bits (double 16-bit arithmetic),
   nx16 bits (multiple 16-bit arithmetic),
or nx8 bits (multiple byte arithmetic).

Additionally, the program could be made to input and output decimal, rather than hexadecimal numbers.

14 Block transfer and search instructions

The Z80 microprocessor has eight very powerful block instructions which allow operations on blocks of consecutive memory bytes. Four of the instructions are block transfer instructions which allow the contents of one block of memory bytes to be transferred to another block of memory; the other four instructions are block search instructions which allow a block of memory bytes to be searched for one of the bytes containing a specified value.

All the block instructions are included in Table C.4 in Appendix C.

14.1 BLOCK TRANSFER INSTRUCTIONS

Suppose it was necessary to move the contents of a block of ten memory bytes, starting at the byte labelled SOURCE, to a block starting at a byte labelled DESTIN. Program 14.1 could be used to perform that function.

```
        ; Program 14.1  block transfer - the hard way
        ;
                LD    HL,SOURCE         ; set up pointers
                LD    DE,DESTIN
                LD    B,10              ; and counter
        ;
NEXBYT:         LD    A,(HL)            ; transfer byte
                LD    (DE),A
        ;
                INC   HL                ; increment pointers
                INC   DE
                DJNZ  NEXBYT            ; and counter
                HALT
        ;
SOURCE:         DEFM  'ABCDEFGHIJ'
DESTIN:         DEFM  '0000000000'
```

The register pairs HL and DE are set to point to the first byte of the source and destination blocks of memory bytes, respectively. The register B is to be used as the counter and is initialised to ten.

74

In the loop, a byte is transferred from the source block of memory bytes to the destination block of memory byts via the accumulator. The register pairs HL and DE are both incremented by one to point to the next bytes in the source and destination blocks of memory bytes.

When the looping finishes and the HALT instruction is executed, the string of the first ten letters of the alphabet will have been moved, character by character, to the ten bytes starting at DESTIN, thereby overwriting the zeros originally contained in those bytes.

Exercise 14.1
Using the BC register pair as a counter, what changes must be made to Program 14.1 to cater for blocks of thousands of memory bytes instead of tens of memory bytes?

The Z80 microprocessor has an instruction which could replace the instructions in the loop in Program 14.1. It is the LDIR instruction - LoaD, Increment and Repeat. Prior to execution of the LDIR instruction, HL must contain the address of the first of the source block memory bytes, DE must contain the first of the destination block memory bytes, and BC must contain the number of bytes to be transferred. Program 14.2 shows a version of Program 14.1 using the LDIR instruction.

```
; Program 14.2 block transfer - the easy way
;
        LD   HL,SOURCE ; set up pointers
        LD   DE,DESTIN
        LD   BC,10      ; and counter
;
        LDIR            ; transfer block
        HALT
;
SOURCE: DEFM 'ABCDEFGHIJ
DESTIN: DEFM '0000000000'
```

Program 14.2 is functionally the same as Program 14.1 except that Program 14.2 allows blocks of up to 64K bytes to be transferred, since a register pair is being used as the counter instead of a single register. For each byte transfer HL and DE are incremented by one and BC is decremented by one - the transfer continues until BC is equal to 0.

The LDDR - LoaD, Decrement and Repeat instruction is the same as the LDIR instruction except that, as its mnemonic suggests, HL and DE are decremented instead of incremented.

Exercise 14.2
Rewrite Program 14.2 using the LDDR instruction instead of the LDIR instruction.

Two other block transfer instructions LDI and LDD are similar to

75

the LDIR and LDDR instructions except that they do not automatically go on to transfer the next byte.

The LDI - LoaD and Increment instruction increments up from the beginning of the block of bytes, whereas the LDD - LoaD and Decrement instruction decrements down from the end of the block of bytes. The LDI insruction transfers a byte, increments both HL and DE by one and decrements BY by one, whereas the LDD instruction, after transferring a byte, decrements both HL and DE by one and decrements BC by one.

It is important to know that the condition of BC becoming zero is indicated by the P/V flag not the zero flag. The P/V flag is set to 0 (PO mnemonic) if BC is zero, otherwise it is set to 1 (PE mnemonic).

Exercise 14.3
Rewrite Program 14.2 using an LDI instruction instead of the LDIR instruction.

The LDIR and LDDR instructions can be used only when the number of bytes to be transferred is known in advance. When the criteria for the numbers of bytes to be transferred are not known in advance, the LDI or LDD instructions must be used and the program must write the instructions to transfer all the bytes.

Exercise 14.4
Write a program segment which moves a block of characters from one place to another. A maximum of one thousand characters in the block should be catered for, although the transfer should stop when a byte containing zero is encountered. The zero byte should not be transferred.

Care must be taken during block transfers when the source and destination blocks overlap. Take, for example, a situation where it is necessary to move a block of bytes so many bytes through memory as is done by the following program segment

```
LD    HL,START
LD    DE,START+100
LD    BC,500
LDIR
```

The first one hundred bytes of the source block of bytes will be copied into the first one hundred bytes of the destination block of bytes which also happens to be the second one hundred bytes of the source block of bytes. So the last four hundred bytes of the source block of bytes are overwritten before they can be transferred to the destination block of bytes.

Exercise 14.5
What change can be made to the program segment above to move the block of bytes down through memory correctly?

14.2   BLOCK SEARCH INSTRUCTIONS

There are four block search instructions which allow a block of
memory bytes to be searched for one of them containing the same
contents as the accumulator. The operation of all four
instructions requires that the accumulator shall contain the byte
contents to be searched for, HL contain the address of the first
byte of the block of bytes to be searched, and BC contain a count
of the number of bytes in the block, all to be set before the
instructions are executed.

As for the block transfer instructions, two of the block search
instructions automatically search through the block and the other
two block search instructions require extra instructions to move
on to the next byte in the block.

The two automatic block search instructions are CPIR – ComPare,
Increment and Repeat and CPDR – ComPare, Decrement and Repeat.
Program 14.3 shows a use of the CPIR instruction in searching
for the value zero in a block of memory bytes.

```
; Program 14.3   search a block for zero
;
;
        LD    HL,START  ; set up pointer,
        LD    BC,10     ; counter
        LD    A,0       ; and accumulator
;
        CPIR            ; search block for zero
;
        LD    A,C       ; output value of counter
        ADD   A,30H
        CALL  COUT
        HALT
;
START:  DEFB 1
        DEFB 2
        DEFB 3
        DEFB 0
        DEFB 4
        DEFB 5
        DEFB 0
        DEFB 6
        DEFB 0
        DEFB 7
```

First of all HL is loaded with the address of the first byte of
the block labelled START, the register pair BC is loaded with the
number of bytes in the block and the accumulator is loaded with
the value to be found.

The CPIR instruction then indexes through the block of bytes
until either a match with the contents of the accumulator is
found or the end of the block is reached, that is, BC becomes
zero. For each byte, the contents of the accumulator are

compared with the contents of the byte; if they are equal the zero flag is set to 1; the HL register pair is incremented by one and the BC register pair is decremented by one. Finally, if the zero flag is set to 1, or BC is zero, the instruction is finished; otherwise the next byte in the block is considered, and so on.

In the same way that the P/V flag is used to indicate that BC contains zero during execution of the LDI and LDD block transfer instructions, so the P/V flag is used to indicate the contents of BC on termination of the block search instructions.

Exercise 14.6
Referring to Program 14.3 what number will be output by the program as it stands and, also, if the block did not contain a zero value? You may find the specification of the CPIR instruction in Table C.4 in Appendix C helpful in answering this question.

The CPDR instruction can be used to search a block from the end back to the beginning. In this case, HL is initially set to point to the last byte of the block of memory bytes and during execution of the instruction HL is decremented, rather than incremented, by one.

The CPI - ComPare and Increment and CPD - ComPare and Decrement instructions are similar to the CPIR and CPDR except that they do not automatically go on to the next byte. Extra instructions have to be used to test for a match between the accumulator and whether the byte has been found - zero flag is set to 1 - and to detect if the whole of the block has been searched - BC is zero and the P/V flag is set to 0. These two instructions are used in place of the CPIR and CPDR instructions when intermediate processing is required and, for example, when more than one occurrence of the value in the accumulator needs to be detected.

Exercise 14.7
What changes must be made to Program 14.3 to make it output the value of the counter at every occurrence of zero?

It is sometimes useful to know the contents of HL and DE when the block instructions LDIR, LDDR, CPIR and CPDR have finished execution.

For the LDIR instruction, HL and DE will be pointing to the bytes immediately following the ends of the blocks.

For the LDDR instruction, HL and DE will be pointing to the bytes immediately preceding the beginning of the blocks.

For the CPIR instruction, HL will be pointing to the byte immediately following the end of the block.

For the CPDR instruction, HL will be pointing to the byte immediately preceding the beginning of the block.

78

14.3   PROGRAM

This program is required to provide an internal filing system
which can hold up to nine records.   Each record contains 20
characters.

The file should be defined at the end of the main program using
the pseudo instruction

    FILE: DEFS 180

So far as the program is concerned, the contents of the records
(the 20 characters) are immaterial.   The program identifies each
record by a record number which is its numerical position in the
file; so the file has records numbered 1 to 9.

A user of the program should be able to input any of the
following

D n	to delete the record numbered n (n is 1 to 9) - following records move up one record position,
I n 20-character-record	to insert the specified record after the record numbered n (n is 0 to 8)- following records move down one record position,
R n 20-character-record	to replace the record numbered n by the specified record (n is 1 to 9),
L	to list the file on the display - for each record, its number and its contents,
F character-string	to find and display the first record in the file containing the specified character-string,which may be 1, 2 or 3 characters.

15   Decimal arithmetic

Up to now, we have only considered the binary representation of numbers in the Z80 microprocessor, and arithmetic has involved signed and unsigned binary numbers. However, the Z80 microprocessor caters for another representation of numbers — Binary Coded Decimal, or BCD for short.

15.1 BCD REPRESENTATION

The Binary Coded Decimal representation of numbers requires that each decimal digit be expressed as a 4-digit binary number, so that 9 would be written as 1001B.

A 4-bit unit is called a nibble, so a nibble is half a byte and a byte can hold a 2-digit BCD number, as follows

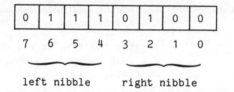

The left nibble, bits 7 to 4, inclusive, contains the BCD number 7 and the right nibble, bits 3 to 0, inclusive, contains the BCD number 4. The byte as a whole contains the BCD number 74.

Exercise 15.1
Give the binary contents of a byte which holds the BCD number 57.

A nibble can contain a BCD number in the range 0 to 9, but an unsigned binary number in the range 0 to 15, so you can see that the BCD representation is wasteful compared to the unsigned binary representation.

Exercise 15.2
Compare the range of BCD and unsigned binary numbers which can be contained in a byte.

Numbers are normally input from the keyboard and output to the display as decimal digits. To enable arithmetic to be performed on the numbers they have to be converted to binary, and then the results converted from binary to decimal before being output. If a computer has instructions which allow arithmetic to be performed with numbers in their decimal digit form then the conversion from decimal to binary, and vice versa, would be unnecessary.

The Z80 microprocessor does have facilities for decimal arithmetic (the Decimal Adjust Accumulator instruction) and facilities for moving nibbles around (the Rotate Left Digit and Rotate Right Digit instructions), so sometimes it is more convenient to use the BCD representation of numbers rather than their binary representation.

15.2 BCD ARITHMETIC

As you would expect, BCD arithmetic is not as straightforward as binary arithmetic on a computer which is binary orientated. The standard arithmetic instructions cannot be used because they are binary and, therefore, not suitable for BCD arithmetic. For example, the sum of BCD 28 and BCD 39, would yield the incorrect result of BCD 61, if a standard binary add operation were to be used, as follows

```
    00101000      BCD 28
  + 00111001      BCD 39
    --------
    01100001      BCD 61 - incorrect
    --------
```

The error occurs because, in BCD arithmetic, if the sum of the right nibbles is greater than 9 a carry into the left nibble is required. Binary arithmetic also produces nibbles containing numbers in the range 1010B to 1111B for which there is no valid BCD equivalent.

Having performed a binary add operation on two BCD numbers it is possible to correct the erroneous result to give a correct BCD result. The correction after the addition of two BCD digits is as follows: if the nibble contains a value between 1010B and 1111B, inclusive, or a carry occurred from the most significant bit of the nibble then 0110B must be added to the nibble, otherwise nothing need be done. The two following examples show the effect of the correction

```
    0110          BCD 6
  + 0111          BCD 7
    ----
    1101          -incorrect BCD result not a BCD digit
  + 0110
    ----
    00010011      BCD 13 - correct BCD result
    --------
```

```
              1000        BCD 8
            + 1001        BCD 9
              ----
            00010001      BCD 11 - incorrect BCD result
          +     0110
            --------
            00010111      BCD 17 - correct BCD result
            --------
```

Exercise 15.3
Show the addition of BCD 17 and BCD 69 as above.

A carry occurring from the left nibble of a 2-digit BCD addition
would indicate overflow, that is, a value greater than 99.

When subtracting one BCD number from another, 0110B must be
subtracted from the result if either a borrow has occurred into
the nibble or the nibble contains a value in the range 1010B to
1111B, inclusive.

Exercise 15.4
Show the subtraction of BCD 56 from BCD 82.

A borrow occurring into the left nibble of a 2-digit BCD
subtraction would indicate overflow.

15.3 THE DAA INSTRUCTION

In order to provide decimal arithmetic a computer must either
provide a separate set of decimal arithmetic instructions, such
as decimal Add, or provide a means of changing a binary
arithmetic result into a decimal arithmetic as shown in the
previous section. The Z80 microprocessor designers chose the
latter by including in the Z80 instruction set the DAA - Decimal
Adjust Accumulator - instruction.

Whenever an arithmetic instruction is executed the two flags in
the flag register which we have not considered so far - the half-
carry and subtract flags - are affected in the following way.

The half-carry flag is set to 1 if an add instruction produces a
carry out of the right nibble of a register, otherwise the flag
is set to 0. Also, the half-carry flag is set to 1 if a subtract
instruction requires a borrow into the right nibble of a
register, otherwise the flag is set to 0.

The subtract flag is set to 1 if the instruction is an add
instruction or to 0 if it is a subtract instruction.

Although the half-carry and subtract flags are used only by the
DAA instruction they are set accordingly after every arithmetic
instruction. Neither of these flags may be used by a programmer
because there are no instructions to set or test them directly.

Using the setting of the half-carry and subtract flas, the DAA

82

instruction corrects the contents of the accumulator, if
necessary, to give a result in the accumulator as if the previous
arithmetic instruction had been a BCD one. For example, the
program segment

```
LD   A,43H
LD   B,28H
ADD  A,B
DAA
```

loads the accumulator and B register with BCD 43 and BCD 28,
respectively, sums them using a binary ADD instruction, and then
adjusts the result to BCD representation using the DAA
instruction. Notice that hexadecimal representation, being a 4-
bit representation, is very useful for writing BCD constants in
programs.

Exercise 15.5
What will be the contents of the accumulator in hexadecimal
after execution of each of the instructions in the program
segment above?

The DAA instruction is used during BCD arithmetic after the
instructions ADD A, SUB, INC A, DEC A, CP, NEG, ADC A, SBC and
the four block search instructions. Notice that the DAA
instructions operate on the accumulator only.

The two flags of most importance to the programmer, which are set
by the DAA instruction, are the carry flag indicating BCD
arithmetic overflow and the zero flag indicating a zero BCD
value. The carry flag setting can also be used in multi-byte BCD
arithmetic, as we shall see later.

15.4   THE DIGIT ROTATE INSTRUCTIONS

Two Z80 instructions are available for rotating nibbles, or BCD
digits - one to rotate to the left and the other to rotate to the
right.

The rotation involves the right nibble of the accumulator and the
two nibbles of a memory byte pointed to by the HL register pair.
The Rotate Left Digit instruction, RLD, operates as follows

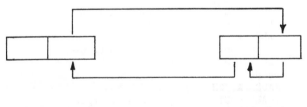

             accumulator   memory byte

The right nibble of the accumulator moves to the right nibble of
the memory byte. The right nibble of the memory byte moves to

the left nibble of the memory byte and the left byte of the
memory byte moves to the right nibble of the accumulator. The
left nibble of the accumulator is not affeced by the rotation.

The Rotate Right Digit instruction, RRD, operates as follows

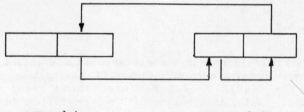

accumulator   memory byte

The RLD and RRD instructions are very useful for manipulating BCD
numbers. For example, look at Program 15.1 which inputs two 2-
digit BCD numbers, adds them, and outputs their sum.

```
        ; Program 15.1  add two 2-digit BCD numbers
        ;
                LD    HL,NUM
                CALL  CINEKO      ; input 1st digit of first number
                AND   0FH
                LD    (HL),A
                CALL  CINEKO      ; input 2nd digit of first number
                AND   0FH
                RLD               ; store first number in NUM
                INC   HL
                CALL  CINEKO      ; input 1st digit of second number
                SUB   30H
                LD    (HL),A
                CALL  CINEKO      ; input 2nd digit of second number
                SUB   30H
                RLD               ; store second number in NUM+1
                LD    HL,NUM
                LD    A,(HL)
                INC   HL
                ADD   A,(HL)      ; add the two numbers
                DAA               ; decimal adjust for BCD
                LD    HL,SUM      ; save result
                LD    (HL),A
                LD    A,0         ; output result
                RLD
                ADD   A,30H
                CALL  COUT        ; - first digit
                LD    A,0
                RLD
                ADD   A,30H
                CALL  COUT        ; - second digit
                HALT
        ;
NUM:            DEFS  2
SUM:            DEFS  1
```

84

Working through the program, the first number is input, digit by digit, and stored in NUM using an RLD instruction, followed by the input of the second number into NUM+1 using another RLD instruction. The HL register pair must be used to point to the memory bytes because the RLD instruction assumes that it does.

The two numbers are then added and immediately adjusted for BCD arithmetic using the DAA instruction. The result is stored before being output, digit by digit, using an RLD instruction to move each nibble in turn from SUM to the accumulator ready for output. Notice that the accumulator has to be set to zero before the last two RLD instructions are executed — this is to ensure that the left nibble of the accumulator is zero. Although the left nibble is not involved in the decimal rotate instruction, and partly because it is not, you must ensure that the contents of the left nibble of the accumulator are what you want them to be.

15.5 PROGRAM

A program which inputs, adds, subtracts and outputs signed multiple-digit BCD numbers is required.

A BCD number is assumed to be held internally as follows: an initial byte specifies the sign of the number (bit 7 is 0 for a positive number or 1 for a negative number) and the number of BCD digits contained in the number (bits 6 to 0); subsequent bytes contain the BCD digits packed two to a byte.

Write a subroutine called INBCD which inputs a signed BCD number (no sign implies a positive number) from the keyboard and stores it as specified above. On entry to the subroutine the HL register pair points to the first of the bytes where the number is to be stored.

Write a subroutine called OUTBCD which outputs a signed BCD number (suppressed positive sign) to the display. On entry to the subroutine the HL register pair points to the first byte of the number to be output.

Write a subroutine called BCDADD which adds two equal-length signed BCD numbers. On entry to the subroutine the IX and IY register pairs point to the first bytes of the first and second numbers, respectively, and the HL register pair points to the first byte of the resulting number. On exit from the subroutine the accumulator should contain a 1 if overflow occurred, or 0 otherwise.

Write a subroutine called BCDSUB which is similar to the above add subroutine except that the subroutine subtracts the second number from the first number.

Use the subroutines to write a main program which repeatedly inputs two signed BCD numbers separated by either a + character

or a - character and followed by an equal character, and outputs
the result. The program should cater for BCD numbers containing
up to twenty BCD digits.

16 Miscellaneous instructions

There are several instructions which have not yet been considered because they are rarely used or because they are beyond the scope of this book. However, for completeness, they are discussed briefly in this final chapter.

16.1 THE NOP INSTRUCTION

The NOP instruction performs No OPeration but, paradoxically, does have some uses. For example, the instruction can be used to provide a delay in a sequence of code by inserting the instructions

```
DELAY:  NOP
        DJNZ DELAY
```

which will cause a delay of (N - 1) x (4 + 13) + 8 clock periods. (N is the value in the B register prior to the delay loop; the NOP instruction takes 4 clock periods and the DJNZ instruction takes 13 clock periods if B is not zero and 8 clock periods if B is zero.)

16.2 THE AUXILIARY REGISTERS

The Z80 microprocessor has another set of eight registers called the auxiliary registers which are denoted by A', F', B', C', D', E', H' and L'. These auxiliary registers can be used in exactly the same way as their counterparts, but not at the same time.

To change over from using the standard registers to using the auxiliary registers, the instruction

```
EXX      ; exchange standard and auxiliary registers
```

must be executed, causing subsequent instructions to refer to the auxilliary registers. To revert back to using the standard registers another EXX instruction must be executed.

Most programs need to use only the standard registers and to exchange all eight registers would not be necessary. However, for the more frequent requirement that a second accumulator is sometimes necessary, the instruction

```
    EX    AF,AF',  ; exchange AF and AF'
```

is available which interchanges the standard and auxiliary
accumulator and flag registers.

16.3   INPUT AND OUTPUT INSTRUCTIONS

There are twelve input and output instructions altogether and
these are specified in Table C.12 of Appendix C. We have used
two of these instructions, the IN A,(n) and OUT (n),A
instructions, to input and output data to and from the
accumulator.

Input and output of data can be specified to be to and from any
of the single registers using the IN r,(C) and OUT (R),r
instructions, in which case the contents of the C register
identify the port to be used.

The remaining input and output instructions allow the input and
output of blocks of data. These instructions, and their
variations, are similar to the block search instructions except
that, instead of comparing a data byte, a data byte is input or
output. (Also, only the single B register is used as a counter -
not the BC register pair.)

These block input and output instructions appear very useful at
first sight, but it must be remembered that the repeat ones can
be used only with devices which operate at the same high speed as
instructions, which does not include, for example, displays or
keyboards.

16.4   INTERRUPT INSTRUCTIONS

An interrupt facility allows signals from outside to interrupt
the sequence of instructions in the central processing unit.

Five of the instructions associaed with the Z80 interrupt
facility are specified in Table C.8 in Appendix C. The Z80
microprocessor has three modes of interrupt which can be set by
instruction using one of the three IM 0, IM 1 and IM 2
instructions which set the interrupt mode to modes 0, 1 or 2,
respectively. The DI and EI instructions Disable Interrupts and
Enable Interrupts and, therefore, allow interrupts to be disabled
or enabled under program control.

Interrupts are dealt with by Interrupt Service Routines - normal
program segments with a specific function of dealing with a
particular interrupt. The last instruction of an interrupt
service routine is either a RETI (RETurn from Interrupt) or RETN
(RETurn from Non-maskable interrupt) instruction which causes a
return back to the sequence of instructions which was
interrupted. The RETI and RETN instructions are included in
Table C.11 in Appendix C along with the RST (ReSTart) instruction
which is used to service a mode 0 interrupt.

Appendix A Binary and hexadecimal number systems

In order to understand how information is stored in the memory of a computer we need to know about binary and hexadecimal numbers. In everyday life we normally use decimal numbers. However, computers store information in binary, and hexadecimal is a compact way of representing binary.

Put simply, decimal is counting in tens, binary is counting in twos and hexadecimal is counting in sixteens.

A.1 BINARY AND HEXADECIMAL NUMBERS

A decimal number, say 453 may be expressed in the following way

$$453 = (4 \times 10^2) + (5 \times 10^1) + (3 \times 10^0)$$

Similarly, a hexadecimal number, say 974, is expressed as

$$974H = (9 \times 16^2) + (7 \times 16^1) + (4 \times 16^0)$$

and the binary number 101 is expressed as

$$101B = (1 \times 2^2) + (0 \times 2^1) + (1 \times 2^0)$$

The H at the end of the hexadecimal number 974 is there to indicate that that number is, in fact, hexadecimal rather than decimal or binary. Similarly, a binary number is postfixed by the letter B.

Looking at the three numbers above you can see that decimal numbers are expressed in terms of the powers of tens, hexadecimal numbers are expressed in terms of the powers of sixteens and binary numbers are expressed in terms of the powers of two. The ten, sixteen and two are said to be the base or radix, of the numbers. Decimal numbers have a base of ten, hexadecimal numbers a base of sixteen and binary numbers a base of two. Any number can be used as a base, but in computing, and particularly for microprocessors, the most common bases are sixteen and two.

Exercise A.1
By working out the expressions above, what are 974H and 101B equivalent to as decimal numbers?

You know already that decimal numbers use the digits 0 to 9, that is, zero through to one less than the base value.

Exercise A.2
Which digits do binary numbers use?

Hexadecimal numbers need to use sixteen, that is 0 to something. We can use the same digits as are used for decimal numbers up to 9 but for the remaining six digits we need single-character symbols. The chosen symbols are the letters A, B, C, D, E and F, so that hexadecimal A is equivalent to decimal 10 and hexadecimal F is equivalent to decimal 15.

Look now at Figure A.1 which shows the equivalent hexadecimal and binary numbers of the decimal numbers 0 to 15.

decimal	hexadecimal	binary
0	0	0000
1	1	0001
2	2	0010
3	3	0011
4	4	0100
5	5	0101
6	6	0110
7	7	0111
8	8	1000
9	9	1001
10	A	1010
11	B	1011
12	C	1100
13	D	1101
14	E	1110
15	F	1111

Figure A.1

You will need to know the hexadecimal and binary numbers in Figure A.1 by heart, so spend a short time making sure that you know them without having to think about it - especially the binary numbers.

Exercise A.3
What is the decimal equivalent of E8A5H?

A.2   BINARY AND HEXADECIMAL ARITHMETIC

Addition and subtraction can be done using any base. The technique is the same as for decimal numbers except that any reference to ten is replaced by a reference to the base. For example, when adding two hexadecimal numbers, a carry is produced when the addition of two of the digits result in a number greater than FH, (or decimal 15).

Examples of addition and subtraction using hexadecimal and binary numbers are

```
    3A7FH          10110110B
  + 10BBH        - 01011010B
    ----           ---------
    4B3AH          01011100B
    ----           ---------
```

Exercise A.4
Do the following arithmetic

```
    C7BAH          01101101B
  - 9FF8H        + 01011110B
    ----           ---------

    ----           ---------
```

A.3   DECIMAL TO HEXADECIMAL CONVERSION

To convert a decimal number to a hexadecimal number, repeatedly
divide the decimal number by 16 until a 0 quotient is obtained.
The remainders from the divisions constitute the equivalent
hexadecimal number, the last remainder so obtained being the most
significant digit of the hexadecimal number. For example, the
conversion of 745 to hexadecimal looks like

```
16 | 745
16 |  46   remainder 9
16 |   2   remainder E
       0   remainder 2
```

the equivalent hexadecimal number being 2E9H.

Exercise A.5
Convert the decimal number 1582 to hexadecimal.

A.4   HEXADECIMAL TO DECIMAL CONVERSION

To convert a hexadecimal number to a decimal number just expand
the hexadecimal number in powers of 16, and then add the terms.
For example, the conversion of 3AB2H to its equivalent decimal
number would look like

$$3AB2H = (3 \times 16^3)\ (10 \times 16^2) + (11 \times 16^1) + (2 \times 16^0)$$

$$= (3 \times 4096) + (10 \times 256) + (11 \times 16) + (2 \times 1)$$

$$= 12288 + 2560 + 176 + 2$$

$$= 15026$$

the equivalent decimal number being 15026.

A quicker way to convert a hexadecimal number to a decimal number (and vice-versa) is to use a conversion table, assuming that one is readily available.

Exercise A.6
Using the converion tables in Appendix B, convert FBH and A3B2H to decimal and 142 and 9467 to hexadecimal.

A.5   BINARY-HEXADECIMAL CONVERSION

Binary to hexadecimal conversion and hexadecimal to binary conversion is based on the fact that one hexadecimal digit can be replaced by four binary digits and vice-versa.

So to convert a hexadecimal number, say 6BH, to binary, just replace each hexadecimal digit by its four digit binary equivalent - according to the values in Figure A.1.   Hence,

$$6BH = 0110 \ 1011$$

which is equal to   1101011B

with the leading zero removed and the two sets of binary digits joined together.

To convert a binary number to a hexdecimal number, the binary number is separated into groups of four binary digits from the right.   For example, the binary number 1111100111 would look like

$$11 \ 1110 \ 0111$$

Each group of bits is then converted to its equivalent hexadecimal digit, so the binary number above would look like

$$3 \quad E \quad 7$$

Hence, 1111100111B is equivalent to 3E7H.

Exercise A.7
Convert 9AB3H to binary and 110011101111B to hexadecimal.

A.6   DECIMAL-BINARY CONVERSIONS

Conversions between decimal and binary numbers can be done in the same way as we did decimal and hexadecimal number conversions, except that 2 is used wherever we used 16.

However, those methods of conversion are rather tedious for decimal/binary conversions so, either

use hexadecimal as an intermediary, so that, for example, to convert from decimal to binary first convert from decimal to hexadecimal and then to binary, or   use a conversion table.

Exercise A.8
Convert 1290 to binary and 101110111101B to decimal using both
suggested methods.

A.7   BYTES

The basic unit of data in the Z80 microprocessor is a byte, which
contains eight binary digits (bits, for short) or two hexadecimal
digits. The contents (0's and 1's) of a byte may represent any
one of several entities, such as

                a character,
                a number (unsigned),
        or   a signed number.

Representation of characers is dealt with in Chapter 3.

Representation of a number in a byte refers to the contents of a
byte being considered to be the value of the binary number
contained in the byte. For example, a byte containing 01100110B
represents the number 11100110B, 66H or 102 decimal. The range
of numbers which can be contained in a byte is 0 to 11111111B
(FFHand 255 decimal). When it is necessary to do so, this
representation is distinguished from another representation by
referring to it as the unsigned number representation.

Exercise A.9
What range of unsigned numbers can be represented in two bytes
(that is, 16 bits)?

A.8   SIGNED (2's COMPLEMENT) NUMBERS

Numbers which may have negative values as well as positive values
are held in computers in what is called '2's complement form'.
This form of representation depends on numbers consisting of a
fixed number of digits. As we are concerned with the Z80
microprocessor we will consider 2's complement numbers consisting
of eight binary digits.

In the 2's complement system, a negative number is represented by
taking the 2's complement of its equivalent positive value; this
is done by converting all 0's to 1's and 1's to 0's, and then
adding 1. For example,

                +5   is   00000101B

so   -5   is   11111010B
                            + 1

                            11111011B

Hence, -5 is held as 11111011B in a register or memory byte. The mechanism for producing a negative number in 2's complement form is equivalent to subtracting the equivalent positive value from 2.

Exercise A.10
Calculate the binary equivalent of -1, -2 and -126 and the decimal equivalent of 10000000B and 10000001B, assuming an 8-bit 2's complement system.

When performing arithmetic with numbers within a 2's complement system, numbers are added bit by bit as normal but any carry out of the most significant bit is ignored. For example, adding +5 and -5 looks like

```
          00000101B      +5
     +    11111011B    + -5
          ---------      --
    [1]   00000000B       0
          ---------      --
```

The one carry out of the addition of the eight two bits is ignored and the result is contained in the 8 bits - that is, zero, which you would expect to obtain when adding -5 to +5.

Exercise A.11
Calculate -60 + 70, -23 + -46, 85 - 96 and 5 - -121, in binary using an 8-bit 2's complement system.

The range of numbers which can be held in a byte, using 2's complement, goes from -128 to +127 as follows

-128	10000000
-127	10000001
:	:
-2	11111110
-1	11111111
0	00000000
+1	00000001
+2	00000010
:	:
+126	01111110
+127	01111111

There are other ways of representing negative numbers in computers, but the 2's complement method is the most common and the one used by the Z80 microprocessor. However, rather than using the inelegant phrase '2's complement' we shall refer to 'signed numbers' rather than 2's complement numbers from now on.

It may help you in your understanding of signed numbers and unsigned numbers to look at the weighting of the bits in a byte for each of the representations. They are

unsigned numbers	128	64	32	16	8	4	2	1
signed numbers	-128	64	32	16	8	4	2	1

so that, for example, the unsigned number 10010001B is equivalent to

1 x 128 + 1 x 16 + 1 x 1 which equals 145

whereas, the signed number 10010001B is equivalent to

1 x -128 + 1 x 16 + 1 x 1 which equals -111.

Appendix B Hexadecimal-decimal conversion tables

The table below provides for direct conversion between hexadecimal numbers in the range 0 to FF and decimal numbers in the range 0 to 255.

	0	1	2	3	4	5	6	7	8	9	A	B	C	D	E	F
00	000	001	002	003	004	005	006	007	008	009	010	011	012	013	014	015
10	016	017	018	019	020	021	022	023	024	025	026	027	028	029	030	031
20	032	033	034	035	036	037	038	039	040	041	042	043	044	045	046	047
30	048	049	050	051	052	053	054	055	056	057	058	059	060	061	062	063
40	064	065	066	067	068	069	070	071	072	073	074	075	076	077	078	079
50	080	081	082	083	084	085	086	087	088	089	090	091	092	093	094	095
60	096	097	098	099	100	101	102	103	104	105	106	107	108	109	110	111
70	112	113	114	115	116	117	118	119	120	121	122	123	124	125	126	127
80	128	129	130	131	132	133	134	135	136	137	138	139	140	141	142	143
90	144	145	146	147	148	149	150	151	152	153	154	155	156	157	158	159
A0	160	161	162	163	164	165	166	167	168	169	170	171	172	173	174	175
B0	176	177	178	179	180	181	182	183	184	185	186	187	188	189	190	191
C0	192	193	194	195	196	197	198	199	200	201	202	203	204	205	206	207
D0	208	209	210	211	212	213	214	215	216	217	218	219	220	221	222	223
E0	224	225	226	227	228	229	230	231	232	233	234	235	236	237	238	239
F0	240	241	242	243	244	245	246	247	248	249	250	251	252	253	254	255

For conversion of larger numbers use the following in conjuction with the table above.

Hexadecimal	Decimal
100	256
200	512
300	768
400	1024
500	1280
600	1536
700	1792
800	2048
900	2304
A00	2560
B00	2816
C00	3072
D00	3328
E00	3584
F00	3840
1000	4096
2000	8192
3000	12288
4000	16384
5000	20480
6000	24576
7000	28672
8000	32768
9000	36864
A000	40960
B000	45056
C000	49152
D000	53248
E000	57344
F000	61440

Appendix C Summary of Z80 instructions

This appendix contains a summary of the complete Z80 instruction set.

The first table, C.1, gives a summary of the flag operations.

In tables C.2 to C.12, the instructions are logically arranged into functional groups. Each table shows the assembly language mnemonic OP code, the numeric OP code, the symbolic operation, the content of the flag register following the execution of each instruction, the number of bytes required for each instruction as well as the number of memory cycles and the total number of T states (external clock periods) required for the fetching and execution of each instruction. Care has been taken to make each table self-explanatory without requiring any cross reference with the text or other tables.

The following pages have been reproduced by permission of Zilog, Inc. 1977. This material shall not be reproduced without the written consent of Zilog, Inc.

Instruction	C	Z	P/V	S	N	H	Comments
ADD A, s; ADC A,s	‡	‡	V	‡	0	‡	8-bit add or add with carry
SUB s; SBC A, s, CP s, NEG	‡	‡	V	‡	1	‡	8-bit subtract, subtract with carry, compare and negate accumulator
AND s	0	‡	P	‡	0	1	Logical operations
OR s; XOR s	0	‡	P	‡	0	0	And set's different flags
INC s	•	‡	V	‡	0	‡	8-bit increment
DEC m	•	‡	V	‡	1	‡	8-bit decrement
ADD DD, ss	‡	•	•	•	0	X	16-bit add
ADC HL, ss	‡	‡	V	‡	0	X	16-bit add with carry
SBC HL, ss	‡	‡	V	‡	1	X	16-bit subtract with carry
RLA; RLCA, RRA, RRCA	‡	•	•	•	0	0	Rotate accumulator
RL m; RLC m; RR m; RRC m SLA m; SRA m; SRL m	‡	‡	P	‡	0	0	Rotate and shift location m
RLD, RRD	•	‡	P	‡	0	0	Rotate digit left and right
DAA	‡	‡	P	‡	•	‡	Decimal adjust accumulator
CPL	•	•	•	•	1	1	Complement accumulator
SCF	1	•	•	•	0	0	Set carry
CCF	‡	•	•	•	0	X	Complement carry
IN r, (C)	•	‡	P	‡	0	0	Input register indirect
INI; IND; OUTI; OUTD	•	‡	X	X	1	X	Block input and output
INIR; INDR; OTIR; OTDR	•	1	X	X	1	X	Z = 0 if B ≠ 0 otherwise Z = 1
LDI, LDD	•	X	‡	X	0	0	Block transfer instructions
LDIR, LDDR	•	X	0	X	0	0	P/V = 1 if BC ≠ 0, otherwise P/V = 0
CPI, CPIR, CPD, CPDR	•	‡	‡	‡	1	X	Block search instructions Z = 1 if A = (HL), otherwise Z = 0 P/V = 1 if BC ≠ 0, otherwise P/V = 0
LD A, I; LD A, R	•	‡	IFF	‡	0	0	The content of the interrupt enable flip-flop (IFF) is copied into the P/V flag
BIT b, s	•	‡	X	X	0	1	The state of bit b of location s is copied into the Z flag
NEG	‡	‡	V	‡	1	‡	Negate accumulator

The following notation is used in this table:

Symbol	Operation
C	Carry/link flag. C=1 if the operation produced a carry from the MSB of the operand or result.
Z	Zero flag. Z=1 if the result of the operation is zero.
S	Sign flag. S=1 if the MSB of the result is one.
P/V	Parity or overflow flag. Parity (P) and overflow (V) share the same flag. Logical operations affect this flag with the parity of the result while arithmetic operations affect this flag with the overflow of the result. If P/V holds parity, P/V=1 if the result of the operation is even, P/V=0 if result is odd. If P/V holds overflow, P/V=1 if the result of the operation produced an overflow.
H	Half-carry flag. H=1 if the add or subtract operation produced a carry into or borrow from into bit 4 of the accumulator.
N	Add/Subtract flag. N=1 if the previous operation was a subtract.
	H and N flags are used in conjunction with the decimal adjust instruction (DAA) to properly correct the result into packed BCD format following addition or subtraction using operands with packed BCD format.
‡	The flag is affected according to the result of the operation.
•	The flag is unchanged by the operation.
0	The flag is reset by the operation.
1	The flag is set by the operation.
X	The flag is a "don't care."
V	P/V flag affected according to the overflow result of the operation.
P	P/V flag affected according to the parity result of the operation.
r	Any one of the CPU registers A, B, C, D, E, H, L.
s	Any 8-bit location for all the addressing modes allowed for the particular instruction. .
ss	Any 16-bit location for all the addressing modes allowed for that instruction.
ii	Any one of the two index registers IX or IY.
R	Refresh counter.
n	8-bit value in range <0, 255>
nn	16-bit value in range <0, 65535>
m	Any 8-bit location for all the addressing modes allowed for the particular instruction.

Summary of flag operation

Table C.1   Courtesy Zilog, Inc.

Mnemonic	Symbolic Operation	C	Z	P/V	S	N	H	OP-Code 76 543 210	No. of Bytes	No. of M Cycles	No. of T Cycles	Comments
LD r, r′	r ← r′	•	•	•	•	•	•	01 r r′	1	1	4	r, r′ Reg.
LD r, n	r ← n	•	•	•	•	•	•	00 r 110	2	2	7	000 B
								← n →				001 C
LD r, (HL)	r ← (HL)	•	•	•	•	•	•	01 r 110	1	2	7	010 D
LD r, (IX+d)	r ← (IX+d)	•	•	•	•	•	•	11 011 101	3	5	19	011 E
								01 r 110				100 H
								← d →				101 L
LD r, (IY+d)	r ← (IY+d)	•	•	•	•	•	•	11 111 101	3	5	19	111 A
								01 r 110				
								← d →				
LD (HL), r	(HL) ← r	•	•	•	•	•	•	01 110 r	1	2	7	
LD (IX+d), r	(IX+d) ← r	•	•	•	•	•	•	11 011 101	3	5	19	
								01 110 r				
								← d →				
LD (IY+d), r	(IY+d) ← r	•	•	•	•	•	•	11 111 101	3	5	19	
								01 110 r				
								← d →				
LD (HL), n	(HL) ← n	•	•	•	•	•	•	00 110 110	2	3	10	
								← n →				
LD (IX+d), n	(IX+d) ← n	•	•	•	•	•	•	11 011 101	4	5	19	
								00 110 110				
								← d →				
								← n →				
LD (IY+d), n	(IY+d) ← n	•	•	•	•	•	•	11 111 101	4	5	19	
								00 110 110				
								← d →				
								← n →				
LD A, (BC)	A ← (BC)	•	•	•	•	•	•	00 001 010	1	2	7	
LD A, (DE)	A ← (DE)	•	•	•	•	•	•	00 011 010	1	2	7	
LD A, (nn)	A ← (nn)	•	•	•	•	•	•	00 111 010	3	4	13	
								← n →				
								← n →				
LD (BC), A	(BC) ← A	•	•	•	•	•	•	00 000 010	1	2	7	
LD (DE), A	(DE) ← A	•	•	•	•	•	•	00 010 010	1	2	7	
LD (nn), A	(nn) ← A	•	•	•	•	•	•	00 110 010	3	4	13	
								← n →				
								← n →				
LD A, I	A ← I	•	‡	IFF	‡	0	0	11 101 101	2	2	9	
								01 010 111				
LD A, R	A ← R	•	‡	IFF	‡	0	0	11 101 101	2	2	9	
								01 011 111				
LD I, A	I ← A	•	•	•	•	•	•	11 101 101	2	2	9	
								01 000 111				
LD R, A	R ← A	•	•	•	•	•	•	11 101 101	2	2	9	
								01 001 111				

Notes: r, r′ means any of the registers A, B, C, D, E, H, L

   IFF the content of the interrupt enable flip-flop (IFF) is copied into the P/V flag

Flag Notation: • = flag not affected, 0 = flag reset, 1 = flag set, X = flag is unknown,

   ‡ = flag is affected according to the result of the operation.

8-bit load group
Table C.2   Courtesy Zilog, Inc.

Mnemonic	Symbolic Operation	C	Z	P/V	S	N	H	Op-Code 76 543 210	No. of Bytes	No. of M Cycles	No. of T States	Comments
LD dd, nn	dd ← nn	•	•	•	•	•	•	00 dd0 001	3	3	10	dd Pair
								← n →				00 BC
								← n →				01 DE
LD IX, nn	IX ← nn	•	•	•	•	•	•	11 011 101	4	4	14	10 HL
								00 100 001				11 SP
								← n →				
								← n →				
LD IY, nn	IY ← nn	•	•	•	•	•	•	11 111 101	4	4	14	
								00 100 001				
								← n →				
								← n →				
LD HL, (nn)	H ← (nn+1)	•	•	•	•	•	•	00 101 010	3	5	16	
	L ← (nn)							← n →				
								← n →				
LD dd, (nn)	dd_H ← (nn+1)	•	•	•	•	•	•	11 101 101	4	6	20	
	dd_L ← (nn)							01 dd1 011				
								← n →				
								← n →				
LD IX, (nn)	IX_H ← (nn+1)	•	•	•	•	•	•	11 011 101	4	6	20	
	IX_L ← (nn)							00 101 010				
								← n →				
								← n →				
LD IY, (nn)	IY_H ← (nn+1)	•	•	•	•	•	•	11 111 101	4	6	20	
	IY_L ← (nn)							00 101 010				
								← n →				
								← n →				
LD (nn), HL	(nn+1) ← H	•	•	•	•	•	•	00 100 010	3	5	16	
	(nn) ← L							← n →				
								← n →				
LD (nn), dd	(nn+1) ← dd_H	•	•	•	•	•	•	11 101 101	4	6	20	
	(nn) ← dd_L							01 dd0 011				
								← n →				
								← n →				
LD (nn), IX	(nn+1) ← IX_H	•	•	•	•	•	•	11 011 101	4	6	20	
	(nn) ← IX_L							00 100 010				
								← n →				
								← n →				
LD (nn), IY	(nn+1) ← IY_H	•	•	•	•	•	•	11 111 101	4	6	20	
	(nn) ← IY_L							00 100 010				
								← n →				
								← n →				
LD SP, HL	SP ← HL	•	•	•	•	•	•	11 111 001	1	1	6	
LD SP, IX	SP ← IX	•	•	•	•	•	•	11 011 101	2	2	10	
								11 111 001				
LD SP, IY	SP ← IY	•	•	•	•	•	•	11 111 101	2	2	10	
								11 111 001				qq Pair
PUSH qq	(SP-2) ← qq_L	•	•	•	•	•	•	11 qq0 101	1	3	11	00 BC
	(SP-1) ← qq_H											01 DE
PUSH IX	(SP-2) ← IX_L	•	•	•	•	•	•	11 011 101	2	4	15	10 HL
	(SP-1) ← IX_H							11 100 101				11 AF
PUSH IY	(SP-2) ← IY_L	•	•	•	•	•	•	11 111 101	2	4	15	
	(SP-1) ← IY_H							11 100 101				
POP qq	qq_H ← (SP+1)	•	•	•	•	•	•	11 qq0 001	1	3	10	
	qq_L ← (SP)											
POP IX	IX_H ← (SP+1)	•	•	•	•	•	•	11 011 101	2	4	14	
	IX_L ← (SP)							11 100 001				
POP IY	IY_H ← (SP+1)	•	•	•	•	•	•	11 111 101	2	4	14	
	IY_L ← (SP)							11 100 001				

Notes: dd is any of the register pairs BC, DE, HL, SP
qq is any of the register pairs AF, BC, DE, HL
$(PAIR)_H$, $(PAIR)_L$ refer to high order and low order eight bits of the register pair respectively.
E.g. $BC_L = C$, $AF_H = A$

Flag Notation: • = flag not affected, 0 = flag reset, 1 = flag set, X = flag is unknown,
‡ flag is affected according to the result of the operation.

16-bit load group
Table C.3   Courtesy Zilog, Inc.

Mnemonic	Symbolic Operation	C	Z	P/V	S	N	H	76 543 210	No. of Bytes	No. of M Cycles	No. of T States	Comments
EX DE, HL	DE ·· HL	•	•	•	•	•	•	11 101 011	1	1	4	
EX AF, AF'	AF ·· AF'	•	•	•	•	•	•	00 001 000	1	1	4	
EXX	$\begin{pmatrix} BC \\ DE \\ HL \end{pmatrix} \leftrightarrow \begin{pmatrix} BC' \\ DE' \\ HL' \end{pmatrix}$	•	•	•	•	•	•	11 011 001	1	1	4	Register bank and auxiliary register bank exchange
EX (SP), HL	$H \leftrightarrow (SP+1)$ $L \leftrightarrow (SP)$	•	•	•	•	•	•	11 100 011	1	5	19	
EX (SP), IX	$IX_H \leftrightarrow (SP+1)$ $IX_L \leftrightarrow (SP)$	•	•	•	•	•	•	11 011 101 11 100 011	2	6	23	
EX (SP), IY	$IY_H \leftrightarrow (SP+1)$ $IY_L \leftrightarrow (SP)$	•	•	•	•	•	•	11 111 101 11 100 011	2	6	23	
LDI	$(DE) \leftarrow (HL)$ $DE \leftarrow DE+1$ $HL \leftarrow HL+1$ $BC \leftarrow BC-1$	•	•	‡ ①	•	0	0	11 101 101 10 100 000	2	4	16	Load (HL) into (DE), increment the pointers and decrement the byte counter (BC)
LDIR	$(DE) \leftarrow (HL)$ $DE \leftarrow DE+1$ $HL \leftarrow HL+1$ $BC \leftarrow BC-1$ Repeat until $BC = 0$	•	•	0 ①	•	0	0	11 101 101 10 110 000	2 2	5 4	21 16	If BC ≠ 0 If BC = 0
LDD	$(DE) \leftarrow (HL)$ $DE \leftarrow DE-1$ $HL \leftarrow HL-1$ $BC \leftarrow BC-1$	•	•	‡ ①	•	0	0	11 101 101 10 101 000	2	4	16	
LDDR	$(DE) \leftarrow (HL)$ $DE \leftarrow DE-1$ $HL \leftarrow HL-1$ $BC \leftarrow BC-1$ Repeat until $BC = 0$	•	•	0	•	0	0	11 101 101 10 111 000	2 2	5 4	21 16	If BC ≠ 0 If BC = 0
CPI	$A - (HL)$ $HL \leftarrow HL+1$ $BC \leftarrow BC-1$	•	‡ ②	‡ ①	‡	1	‡	11 101 101 10 100 001	2	4	16	
CPIR	$A - (HL)$ $HL \leftarrow HL+1$ $BC \leftarrow BC-1$ Repeat until $A = (HL)$ or $BC = 0$	•	‡ ②	‡ ①	‡	1	‡	11 101 101 10 110 001	2 2	5 4	21 16	If BC ≠ 0 and A ≠ (HL) If BC = 0 or A = (HL)
CPD	$A - (HL)$ $HL \leftarrow HL-1$ $BC \leftarrow BC-1$	•	‡ ②	‡ ①	‡	1	‡	11 101 101 10 101 001	2	4	16	
CPDR	$A - (HL)$ $HL \leftarrow HL-1$ $BC \leftarrow BC-1$ Repeat until $A = (HL)$ or $BC = 0$	•	‡ ②	‡ ①	‡	1	‡	11 101 101 10 111 001	2 2	5 4	21 16	If BC ≠ 0 and A ≠ (HL) If BC = 0 or A = (HL)

Notes: ① P/V flag is 0 if the result of BC-1 = 0, otherwise P/V = 1
② Z flag is 1 if A = (HL), otherwise Z = 0.

Flag Notation: • = flag not affected, 0 = flag reset, 1 = flag set, X = flag is unknown,
‡ = flag is affected according to the result of the operation.

Exchange group and block transfer and search group

Table C.4   Courtesy Zilog, Inc.

		Flags						Op-Code			No. of Bytes	No. of M Cycles	No. of T States	Comments
Mnemonic	Symbolic Operation	C	Z	P/V	S	N	H	76	543	210				
ADD A, r	A ← A + r	↕	↕	V	↕	0	↕	10	[000]	r	1	1	4	r Reg.
ADD A, n	A ← A + n	↕	↕	V	↕	0	↕	11	[000]	110	2	2	7	000 B
								←	n	→				001 C
														010 D
ADD A, (HL)	A ← A + (HL)	↕	↕	V	↕	0	↕	10	[000]	110	1	2	7	011 E
ADD A, (IX+d)	A ← A + (IX+d)	↕	↕	V	↕	0	↕	11	011	101	3	5	19	100 H
								10	[000]	110				101 L
								←	d	→				111 A
ADD A, (IY+d)	A ← A+(IY+d)	↕	↕	V	↕	0	↕	11	111	101	3	5	19	
								10	[000]	110				
								←	d	→				
ADC A, s	A ← A + s + CY	↕	↕	V	↕	0	↕		[001]					s is any of r, n,
SUB s	A ← A − s	↕	↕	V	↕	1	↕		[010]					(HL), (IX+d),
SBC A, s	A ← A − s − CY	↕	↕	V	↕	1	↕		[011]					(IY+d) as shown for
AND s	A ← A ∧ s	0	↕	P	↕	0	1		[100]					ADD instruction
OR s	A ← A ∨ s	0	↕	P	↕	0	0		[110]					The indicated bits
XOR s	A ← A ⊕ s	0	↕	P	↕	0	0		[101]					replace the 000 in
CP s	A − s	↕	↕	V	↕	1	↕		[111]					the ADD set above.
INC r	r ← r + 1	●	↕	V	↕	0	↕	00	r	[100]	1	1	4	
INC (HL)	(HL) ← (HL)+1	●	↕	V	↕	0	↕	00	110	[100]	1	3	11	
INC (IX+d)	(IX+d) ← (IX+d)+1	●	↕	V	↕	0	↕	11	011	101	3	6	23	
								00	110	[100]				
								←	d	→				
INC (IY+d)	(IY+d) ← (IY+d) + 1	●	↕	V	↕	0	↕	11	111	101	3	6	23	
								00	110	[100]				
								←	d	→				
DEC m	m ← m−1	●	↕	V	↕	1	↕			[101]				m is any of r, (HL), (IX+d), (IY+d) as shown for INC. Same format and states as INC. Replace 100 with 101 in OP code.

Notes: The V symbol in the P/V flag column indicates that the P/V flag contains the overflow of the result of the operation. Similarly the P symbol indicates parity. V = 1 means overflow, V = 0 means not overflow. P = 1 means parity of the result is even, P = 0 means parity of the result is odd.

Flag Notation: ● = flag not affected, 0 = flag reset, 1 = flag set, X = flag is unknown,
↕ = flag is affected according to the result of the operation.

8-bit arithmetic and logical group
Table C.5   Courtesy Zilog, Inc.

Mnemonic	Symbolic Operation	Flags						Op-Code	No. of Bytes	No. of M Cycles	No. of T States	Comments
		C	Z	P/V	S	N	H	76 543 210				
DAA	Converts acc. content into packed BCD following add or subtract with packed BCD operands	‡	‡	P	‡	•	‡	00 100 111	1	1	4	Decimal adjust accumulator
CPL	A ← Ā	•	•	•	•	1	1	00 101 111	1	1	4	Complement accumulator (one's complement)
NEG	A ← 0 – A	‡	‡	V	‡	1	‡	11 101 101 / 01 000 100	2	2	8	Negate acc. (two's complement)
CCF	CY ← C̄Y	‡	•	•	•	0	X	00 111 111	1	1	4	Complement carry flag
SCF	CY ← 1	1	•	•	•	0	0	00 110 111	1	1	4	Set carry flag
NOP	No operation	•	•	•	•	•	•	00 000 000	1	1	4	
HALT	CPU halted	•	•	•	•	•	•	01 110 110	1	1	4	
DI	IFF ← 0	•	•	•	•	•	•	11 110 011	1	1	4	
EI	IFF ← 1	•	•	•	•	•	•	11 111 011	1	1	4	
IM 0	Set interrupt mode 0	•	•	•	•	•	•	11 101 101 / 01 000 110	2	2	8	
IM 1	Set interrupt mode 1	•	•	•	•	•	•	11 101 101 / 01 010 110	2	2	8	
IM2	Set interrupt mode 2	•	•	•	•	•	•	11 101 101 / 01 011 110	2	2	8	

Notes: IFF indicates the interrupt enable flip-flop
CY indicates the carry flip-flop.

Flag Notation: • = flag not affected, 0 = flag reset, 1 = flag set, X = flag is unknown,

‡ = flag is affected according to the result of the operation.

General purpose arithmetic and CPU control groups
Table C.6   Courtesy Zilog, Inc.

Mnemonic	Symbolic Operation	C	Z	P/V	S	N	H	Op-Code 76 543 210	No. of Bytes	No. of M Cycles	No. of T States	Comments	
ADD HL, ss	HL ← HL+ss	‡	•	•	•	0	X	00 ss1 001	1	3	11	**ss**	**Reg.**
												00	BC
ADC HL, ss	HL←HL+ ss +CY	‡	‡	V	‡	0	X	11 101 101	2	4	15	01	DE
								01 ss1 010				10	HL
SBC HL, ss	HL←HL - ss -CY	‡	‡	V	‡	1	X	11 101 101	2	4	15	11	SP
								01 ss0 010					
ADD IX, pp	IX ← IX + pp	‡	•	•	•	0	X	11 011 101	2	4	15	**pp**	**Reg.**
								00 pp1 001				00	BC
												01	DE
												10	IX
												11	SP
ADD IY, rr	IY←IY+ rr	‡	•	•	•	0	X	11 111 101	2	4	15	**rr**	**Reg.**
								00 rr1 001				00	BC
												01	DE
												10	IY
												11	SP
INC ss	ss ← ss + 1	•	•	•	•	•	•	00 ss0 011	1	1	6		
INC IX	IX ← IX + 1	•	•	•	•	•	•	11 011 101	2	2	10		
								00 100 011					
INC IY	IY ← IY + 1	•	•	•	•	•	•	11 111 101	2	2	10		
								00 100 011					
DEC ss	ss ← ss - 1	•	•	•	•	•	•	00 ss1 011	1	1	6		
DEC IX	IX ← IX - 1	•	•	•	•	•	•	11 011 101	2	2	10		
								00 101 011					
DEC IY	IY ← IY - 1	•	•	•	•	•	•	11 111 101	2	2	10		
								00 101 011					

Notes: ss is any of the register pairs BC, DE, HL, SP
pp is any of the register pairs BC, DE, IX, SP
rr is any of the register pairs BC, DE, IY, SP.

Flag Notation: • = flag not affected, 0 = flag reset, 1 = flag set, X = flag is unknown,
‡ = flag is affected according to the result of the operation.

16-bit arithmetic group
Table C.7   Courtesy Zilog, Inc.

105

		Flags						Op-Code	No. of Bytes	No. of M Cycles	No. of T States	
Mnemonic	Symbolic Operation	C	Z	P/V	S	N	H	76 543 210				Comments
RLCA		↕	●	●	●	0	0	00 000 111	1	1	4	Rotate left circular accumulator
RLA		↕	●	●	●	0	0	00 010 111	1	1	4	Rotate left accumulator
RRCA		↕	●	●	●	0	0	00 001 111	1	1	4	Rotate right circular accumulator
RRA		↕	●	●	●	0	0	00 011 111	1	1	4	Rotate right accumulator
RLC r		↕	↕	P	↕	0	0	11 001 011 00 000 r	2	2	8	Rotate left circular register r
RLC (HL)		↕	↕	P	↕	0	0	11 001 011 00 000 110	2	4	15	r Reg. 000 B
RLC (IX+d)	r, (HL), (IX+d), (IY+d)	↕	↕	P	↕	0	0	11 011 101 11 001 011 ← d → 00 000 110	4	6	23	001 C 010 D 011 E 100 H 101 L
RLC (IY+d)		↕	↕	P	↕	0	0	11 111 101 11 001 011 ← d → 00 000 110	4	6	23	111 A
RL m	m = r, (HL), (IX+d), (IY+d)	↕	↕	P	↕	0	0	010				Instruction format and states are as shown for RLC,m. To form new OP-code replace 000 of RLC,m with shown code
RRC m	m = r, (HL), (IX+d), (IY+d)	↕	↕	P	↕	0	0	001				
RR m	m = r, (HL), (IX+d), (IY+d)	↕	↕	P	↕	0	0	011				
SLA m	m = r, (HL), (IX+d), (IY+d)	↕	↕	P	↕	0	0	100				
SRA m	m = r, (HL), (IX+d), (IY+d)	↕	↕	P	↕	0	0	101				
SRL m	m = r, (HL), (IX+d), (IY+d)	↕	↕	P	↕	0	0	111				
RLD		●	↕	P	↕	0	0	11 101 101 01 101 111	2	5	18	Rotate digit left and right between the accumulator and location (HL).
RRD		●	↕	P	↕	0	0	11 101 101 01 100 111	2	5	18	The content of the upper half of the accumulator is unaffected

Flag Notation: ● = flag not affected, 0 = flag reset, 1 = flag set, X = flag is unknown,
‡ = flag is affected according to the result of the operation.

Rotate and shift group
Table C.8   Courtesy Zilog, Inc.

Mnemonic	Symbolic Operation	C	Z	P/V	S	N	H	Op-Code 76 543 210	No. of Bytes	No. of M Cycles	No. of T States	Comments	
BIT b, r	$Z \leftarrow \overline{r_b}$	•	‡	X	X	0	1	11 001 011 01 b r	2	2	8	**r**	**Reg.**
BIT b, (HL)	$Z \leftarrow \overline{(HL)_b}$	•	‡	X	X	0	1	11 001 011 01 b 110	2	3	12	000 001 010 011	B C D E
BIT b, (IX+d)	$Z \leftarrow \overline{(IX+d)_b}$	•	‡	X	X	0	1	11 011 101 11 001 011 ← d → 01 b 110	4	5	20	100 101 111	H L A
BIT b, (IY+d)	$Z \leftarrow \overline{(IY+d)_b}$	•	‡	X	X	0	1	11 111 101 11 001 011 ← d → 01 b 110	4	5	20	**b** 000 001 010 011 100 101 110 111	**Bit Tested** 0 1 2 3 4 5 6 7
SET b, r	$r_b \leftarrow 1$	•	•	•	•	•	•	11 001 011 [11] b r	2	2	8		
SET b, (HL)	$(HL)_b \leftarrow 1$	•	•	•	•	•	•	11 001 011 [11] b 110	2	4	15		
SET b, (IX+d)	$(IX+d)_b \leftarrow 1$	•	•	•	•	•	•	11 011 101 11 001 011 ← d → [11] b 110	4	6	23		
SET b, (IY+d)	$(IY+d)_b \leftarrow 1$	•	•	•	•	•	•	11 111 101 11 001 011 ← d → [11] b 110	4	6	23		
RES b, m	$s_b \leftarrow 0$ $m \equiv r, (HL),$ $(IX+d),$ $(IY+d)$							[10]				To form new OP-code replace [11] of SET b,m with [10]. Flags and time states for SET instruction	

Notes: The notation s_b indicates bit b (0 to 7) or location s.

Flag Notation: • = flag not affected, 0 = flag reset, 1 = flag set, X = flag is unknown,
‡ = flag is affected according to the result of the operation.

Bit set, reset and test group
Table C.9   Courtesy Zilog, Inc.

Mnemonic	Symbolic Operation	Flags						Op-Code			No. of Bytes	No. of M Cycles	No. of T States	Comments
		C	Z	P/V	S	N	H	76	543	210				
JP nn	PC ← nn	•	•	•	•	•	•	11	000	011	3	3	10	
								← n →						
								← n →						
JP cc, nn	If condition cc is true PC ←nn, otherwise continue	•	•	•	•	•	•	11	cc	010	3	3	10	
								← n →						
								← n →						
JR e	PC ← PC + e	•	•	•	•	•	•	00	011	000	2	3	12	
								← e-2 →						
JR C, e	If C = 0, continue	•	•	•	•	•	•	00	111	000	2	2	7	If condition not met
								← e-2 →						
	If C = 1, PC ← PC+e										2	3	12	If condition is met
JR NC, e	If C = 1, continue	•	•	•	•	•	•	00	110	000	2	2	7	If condition not met
								← e-2 →						
	If C = 0, PC ← PC + e										2	3	12	If condition is met
JR Z, e	If Z = 0 continue	•	•	•	•	•	•	00	101	000	2	2	7	If condition not met
								← e-2 →						
	If Z = 1, PC ← PC + e										2	3	12	If condition is met
JR NZ, e	If Z = 1, continue	•	•	•	•	•	•	00	100	000	2	2	7	If condition not me
								← e-2 →						
	If Z = 0, PC ← PC + e										2	3	12	If condition met
JP (HL)	PC ← HL	•	•	•	•	•	•	11	101	001	1	1	4	
JP (IX)	PC ← IX	•	•	•	•	•	•	11	011	101	2	2	8	
								11	101	001				
JP (IY)	PC ← IY	•	•	•	•	•	•	11	111	101	2	2	8	
								11	101	001				
DJNZ,e	B ← B-1 If B = 0, continue	•	•	•	•	•	•	00	010	000	2	2	8	If B = 0
								← e-2 →						
	If B ≠ 0, PC ← PC + e										2	3	13	IF B ≠ 0

cc	Condition
000	NZ non zero
001	Z zero
010	NC non carry
011	C carry
100	PO parity odd
101	PE parity even
110	P sign positive
111	M sign negative

Notes: e represents the extension in the relative addressing mode.

e is a signed two's complement number in the range $<-126, 129>$

e-2 in the op-code provides an effective address of pc +e as PC is incremented by 2 prior to the addition of e.

Flag Notation: • = flag not affected, 0 = flag reset, 1 = flag set, X = flag is unknown,

‡ = flag is affected according to the result of the operation.

Jump group
Table C.10   Courtesy Zilog, Inc.

Mnemonic	Symbolic Operation	C	Z	P/V	S	N	H	76 543 210	No. of Bytes	No. of M Cycles	No. of T States	Comments
CALL nn	$(SP-1)\leftarrow PC_H$ $(SP-2)\leftarrow PC_L$ $PC\leftarrow nn$	•	•	•	•	•	•	11 001 101 ← n → ← n →	3	5	17	
CALL cc, nn	If condition cc is false continue, otherwise same as CALL nn	•	•	•	•	•	•	11 cc 100 ← n → ← n →	3 3	3 5	10 17	If cc is false If cc is true
RET	$PC_L\leftarrow(SP)$ $PC_H\leftarrow(SP+1)$	•	•	•	•	•	•	11 001 001	1	3	10	
RET cc	If condition cc is false continue, otherwise same as RET	•	•	•	•	•	•	11 cc 000	1 1	1 3	5 11	If cc is false If cc is true
RETI	Return from interrupt	•	•	•	•	•	•	11 101 101 01 001 101	2	4	14	
RETN	Return from non maskable interrupt	•	•	•	•	•	•	11 101 101 01 000 101	2	4	14	
RST p	$(SP-1)\leftarrow PC_H$ $(SP-2)\leftarrow PC_L$ $PC_H\leftarrow 0$ $PC_L\leftarrow P$	•	•	•	•	•	•	11 t 111	1	3	11	

cc	Condition	
000	NZ	non zero
001	Z	zero
010	NC	non carry
011	C	carry
100	PO	parity odd
101	PE	parity even
110	P	sign positive
111	M	sign negative

t	P
000	00H
001	08H
010	10H
011	18H
100	20H
101	28H
110	30H
111	38H

Flag Notation: • = flag not affected, 0 = flag reset, 1 = flag set, X = flag is unknown
‡ = flag is affected according to the result of the operation.

Call and return group
Table C.11   Courtesy Zilog, Inc.

Mnemonic	Symbolic Operation	C	Z	P/V	S	N	H	Op-Code 76 543 210	No. of Bytes	No. of M Cycles	No. of T States	Comments
IN A, (n)	$A \leftarrow (n)$	●	●	●	●	●	●	11 011 011 ← n →	2	3	11	n to $A_0 \sim A_7$ Acc to $A_8 \sim A_{15}$
IN r, (C)	$r \leftarrow (C)$ if r = 110 only the flags will be affected	●	↕	P	↕	0	↕	11 101 101 01 r 000	2	3	12	C to $A_0 \sim A_7$ B to $A_8 \sim A_{15}$
INI	$(HL) \leftarrow (C)$ ① $B \leftarrow B - 1$ $HL \leftarrow HL + 1$	●	↕	X	X	1	X	11 101 101 10 100 010	2	4	16	C to $A_0 \sim A_7$ B to $A_8 \sim A_{15}$
INIR	$(HL) \leftarrow (C)$ $B \leftarrow B - 1$ $HL \leftarrow HL + 1$ Repeat until B = 0	●	1	X	X	1	X	11 101 101 10 110 010	2 2	5 (If B ≠ 0) 4 (If B = 0)	21 16	C to $A_0 \sim A_7$ B to $A_8 \sim A_{15}$
IND	$(HL) \leftarrow (C)$ ① $B \leftarrow B - 1$ $HL \leftarrow HL - 1$	●	↕	X	X	1	X	11 101 101 10 101 010	2	4	16	C to $A_0 \sim A_7$ B to $A_8 \sim A_{15}$
INDR	$(HL) \leftarrow (C)$ $B \leftarrow B - 1$ $HL \leftarrow HL - 1$ Repeat until B = 0	●	1	X	X	1	X	11 101 101 10 111 010	2 2	5 (If B ≠ 0) 4 (If B = 0)	21 16	C to $A_0 \sim A_7$ B to $A_8 \sim A_{15}$
OUT (n), A	$(n) \leftarrow A$	●	●	●	●	●	●	11 010 011 ← n →	2	3	11	n to $A_0 \sim A_7$ Acc to $A_8 \sim A_{15}$
OUT (C), r	$(C) \leftarrow r$	●	●	●	●	●	●	11 101 101 01 r 001	2	3	12	C to $A_0 \sim A_7$ B to $A_8 \sim A_{15}$
OUTI	$(C) \leftarrow (HL)$ ① $B \leftarrow B - 1$ $HL \leftarrow HL + 1$	●	↕	X	X	1	X	11 101 101 10 100 011	2	4	16	C to $A_0 \sim A_7$ B to $A_8 \sim A_{15}$
OTIR	$(C) \leftarrow (HL)$ $B \leftarrow B - 1$ $HL \leftarrow HL + 1$ Repeat until B = 0	●	1	X	X	1	X	11 101 101 10 110 011	2 2	5 (If B ≠ 0) 4 (If B = 0)	21 16	C to $A_0 \sim A_7$ B to $A_8 \sim A_{15}$
OUTD	$(C) \leftarrow (HL)$ ① $B \leftarrow B - 1$ $HL \leftarrow HL - 1$	●	↕	X	X	1	X	11 101 101 10 101 011	2	4	16	C to $A_0 \sim A_7$ B to $A_8 \sim A_{15}$
OTDR	$(C) \leftarrow (HL)$ $B \leftarrow B - 1$ $HL \leftarrow HL - 1$ Repeat until B = 0	●	1	X	X	1	X	11 101 101 10 111 011	2 2	5 (If B ≠ 0) 4 (If B = 0)	21 16	C to $A_0 \sim A_7$ B to $A_8 \sim A_{15}$

Notes: ① If the result of B - 1 is zero the Z flag is set, otherwise it is reset.

Flag Notation: ● = flag not affected, 0 = flag reset, 1 = flag set, X = flag is unknown,
↕ = flag is affected according to the result of the operation.

Input and output group
Table C.12   Courtesy Zilog, Inc.

Appendix D Display and keyboard character codes

The ASCII code character set is shown below

b4	b3	b2	b1	COL→ ↓ROW	0 0 0	0 0 1	0 1 0	0 1 1	1 0 0	1 0 1	1 1 0	1 1 1
					0	**1**	**2**	**3**	**4**	**5**	**6**	**7**
0	0	0	0	0	NUL	DLE	SP	0	@	P	`	p
0	0	0	1	1	SOH	DC1	!	1	A	Q	a	q
0	0	1	0	2	STX	DC2	"	2	B	R	b	r
0	0	1	1	3	ETX	DC3	# £	3	C	S	c	s
0	1	0	0	4	EOT	DC4	$	4	D	T	d	t
0	1	0	1	5	ENQ	NAK	%	5	E	U	e	u
0	1	1	0	6	ACK	SYN	&	6	F	V	f	v
0	1	1	1	7	BEL	ETB	'	7	G	W	g	w
1	0	0	0	8	BS	CAN	(	8	H	X	h	x
1	0	0	1	9	HT	EM	)	9	I	Y	i	y
1	0	1	0	10	LF	SUB	*	:	J	Z	j	z
1	0	1	1	11	VT	ESC	+	;	K	[	k	{
1	1	0	0	12	FF	FS	,	<	L	\	l	¦
1	1	0	1	13	CR	GS	−	=	M	]	m	}
1	1	1	0	14	SO	RS	.	>	N	^	n	~
1	1	1	1	15	SI	US	/	?	O	_	o	DEL

For example, the ASCII code for the character K is binary 1001011, hexadecimal 4B and decimal 75.

Appendix E   Expression operators

The following table lists these operators which may be used in an operand expression. The list is in order of precedence of evaluation.

OPERATOR	FUNCTION
+	Unary plus
-	Unary minus
.NOT. or \	Logical NOT
.RES.	Result
**	Exponentiation
*	Multiplication
/	Division
.MOD.	Modulo
.SHR.	Logical shift right
.SHL.	Logical shift left
+	Addition
-	Subtraction
.AND. or &	Logical AND
.OR. or ^	Logical OR
.XOR.	Logical XOR
.EQ. or =	Equals
.GT. or >	Greater than (signed)
.LT. or <	Less than (signed)
.UGT.	Unsigned greater than
.ULT.	Unsigned less than

The Result operator (.RES.) causes overflow to be suppressed during evaluation, so that an assembly error does not result from an overflow condition.

The Modulo operator (.MOD.) is defined as

.MOD.B = A-B*(A/B)

where the A/B is an integer division.

The Shift operators (.SHR. and .SHL.) are followed by two arguments. The first argument is shifted by the number of bits specified by the second argument.

The five comparison operators (.EQ., .GT., .LT., .UGT. and .ULT.) evaluate to logical TRUE (all ones) if the comparison is true, and a logical FALSE (zero) otherwise.

Exercise answers

The answers are in exercise-number/chapter-number order. This unusual ordering will help you to avoid seeing the answer to the following exercise.

ANSWERS TO EXERCISES NUMBERED 1

1.1 A keyboard is used to input programs and

2.1 Because the value of n must be contained in one byte.

3.1 ; subroutine to sum the single registers
     ;
     SUMREG: LD   A,0
             ADD   A,B
             ADD   A,C
             ADD   A,D
             ADD   A,E
             ADD   A,H
             ADD   A,L
             RET

4.1 ; program to repeatedly output an *
     ;
              LD   A,'*'
     NEXT: CALL COUT
              JP   NEXT

5.1   A   S   Z
                           -      -   -
              LD   A,120   120   ?   ?
              SUB   122   -2   1   0
              LD   B,A   -2   1   0
              SUB   B   0   0   1
              ADD   A,70   70   0   0
              NEG   -70   1   0

6.1 255

7.1   LD   A,'*'   will be executed   4 times
              CALL COUT   will be executed 24 times
              DEC   C   will be executed   4 times

8.1 Yes

9.1 The Z flag will be set to 1.

10.1 The accumulator and carry flag will contain 53H and 1,
     respectively.

11.1 The result of the logical operator XOR is one if the two
     binary values to be XORed are different, otherwise the
     result is zero.

114

12.1

	A	Carry
RLA	01010110B	1
RLCA	10101100B	0
RRA	01010110B	0
RRCA	00101011B	0

13.1 -32768 to +32767

14.1 Replace LD B,10 by LD BC,number-of-bytes,
     and DJNZ NEXBYT by DEC BC

```
              LD   A,B
              CP   0
              JP   NZ,NEXBYT
              LD   A,C
              CP   0
              JP   NZ,NEXBYT
```

15.1 01010111B

A.1 974H is equivalent to 2420.
     101B is equivalent to 5.

ANSWERS TO EXERCISES NUMBERED 2

1.2 The accumulator and flag registers, respectively.

2.2   LD   A,73
           ADD A,55
           SUB 21

3.2 47H and +.

4.2 A JP instruction occupies 3 bytes and a JR instruction
     occupies 2 bytes.

5.2   i)   LD   A,X
     ii)   SUB 10
    iii)   JP   Z,EQUAL
     iv)   LD   A,0

6.2 ; program to output n asterisks
     ;
              CALL CINEKO   ; input digit
              SUB 30H   ; convert to value n
              LD   B,A
              LD   A,'*'
     NEXTAS: CALL COUT   ; output *
              DJNZ NEXTAS
              HALT

7.2   i) Implied addressing (the accumulator is implied)
      ii) Register addressing (register D)
     iii) Implied addressing (the accumulator is implied) and
          immediate addressing (the value 50)
      iv) Register addressing (register A) and
          extended addressing (the address 6352H)

8.2 CARRY

9.2   BIT 0,A
           JR   Z,EVEN
     ODD: SET 7,B
           JR   CONTIN
     EVEN: RES 7,B
     CONTIN: -

10.2

		B	C	Carry
		-	-	-----
LD	B,11	00001011B (+10)	?	?
SRA	B	00000101B (+5)	?	1
LD	C,-8	"	11111000B (-8)	1
SRA	C	"	11111100B (-4)	0

116

11.2

		A	S	Z	C
		-	-	-	-
LD	A,10110101B	10110101B	?	?	?
LD	C,11110000B	10110101B	?	?	?
AND	00011111B	00010101B	0	0	0
OR	C	11110101B	1	0	0
XOR	11001100B	00111001B	0	0	0
CPL		11000110B	0	0	0

12.2 The accumulator rotate instructions each occupy one byte
and set only the carry, flag whereas the general register
and memory byte rotate instructions each occupy two or four
bytes and set the carry, zero and sign flags.

13.2 RESMS will contain 0668H and RESLS will contain 0930H.

14.2
```
        LD   HL,SOURCE+9   ; set pointers to the end
        LD   DE,DESTIN+9   ; of the blocks
        LD   BC,10
        LDDR
        HALT
```

15.2 A byte can contain BCD numbers in the range 0 to 99 and
unsigned binary numbers in the range 0 to 255, that is,
more than double the range for BCD numbers.

A.2 0 and 1.

1.3 Decimal 65536, hexadecimal 10000.

2.3
```
        LD    A,56
        SUB   22
        LD    B,A
        ADD   A,B
        ADD   A,B
```

3.3 1008H

4.3
```
; subroutine to input and echo a character
;
CINEKO: CALL  CIN
        CALL  COUT
        RET
```

5.3
```
; program to check for B + C being +ve, -ve or 0
;
        LD    A,B
        ADD   A,C       ; B + C
        JP    M,NEG
        JP    Z,ZERO
        LD    A,'P'      ; +ve
        CALL  COUT
        JP    DONE
NEG:    LD    A,'N'      ; -ve
        CALL  COUT
        JP    DONE
ZERO:   LD    A,'Z'      ; 0
        CALL  COUT
DONE:   -
```

6.3
```
; program to output digits 9 to 1
;
        LD    A,39H      ; code for 9
NEXDIG: CALL  COUT
        DEC   A
        CP    30H
        JR    NZ,NEXDIG
        HALT
```

7.3

		A	HL
		-	--
LD	HL,N2	?	1761H
LD	A,(N1)	14H	1761H
SUB	(HL)	37H	1761H
LD	(DIFF),A	37H	1761H
LD	A,(N1)	14H	1761H
ADD	A,(HL)	F1H	1761H
LD	(SUM),A	F1H	1761H
HALT		F1H	1761H

```
8.3             SCF              ; set carry flag to 1
                CCF              ; complement it (now set to 0)

9.3    161H

10.3            SLA  A       ; 2 x N
                LD   B,A
                SLA  A       ; 2 x (2 x N)
                SLA  A       ; 2 x (2 x 2 x N)
                ADD  A,B     ; 2 x 2 x 2 x N + 2 x N

11.3            OR   30H

12.3            LD   A,B
                RRCA
                OR   C
                LD   (SEXAGE),A

13.3            SCF          ; reset carry flag
                CCF          ; to 0
                SUB  HL,BC

14.3            LD   HL,SOURCE
                LD   DE,DESTIN
                LD   BC,10
        NEXBYT: LDI
                JP   PE,NEXBYT
                HALT

15.3            00010111     BCD 17
             +  01101001     BCD 69
                --------
                10000000
                  + 0110
                --------
                10000110     BCD 86
                --------
```

A.3 E8A5H = E x 4096 + 8 x 256 + A x 16 + 5 x 1
           = 14 x 4096 + 8 x 256 + 10 x 16 + 5 x 1
           = 57344 + 2048 + 160 + 5
           = 59557

ANSWERS TO EXERCISES NUMBERED 4

1.4 Hexadecimal B0

2.4   27   1BH
     -27   E5H
     -26   E6H

4.4 37H and 08H

5.4   LD   A,(COUNT)
             CP   100
             JP   M,LESS   ; COUNT < 100
             JP   Z,EQUAL   ; COUNT = 100
             JP   GREAT   ; COUNT > 100

6.4   A   B   C   D   E   SP
                             -    -   -   -   -   --
             LD   A,0AH   0AH ?   ?   ?   ?   ?
             LD   B,0BH   0AH 0BH ?   ?   ?   ?
             LD   C,0CH   0AH 0BH 0CH ?   ?   ?
             LD   D,0DH   0AH 0BH 0CH 0DH ?   ?
             LD   E,0EH   0AH 0BH 0CH 0DH 0EH ?
             LD   SP,16383 0AH 0BH 0CH 0DH 0EH 16383
             PUSH AF   0AH 0BH 0CH 0DH 0EH 16381
             PUSH BC   0AH 0BH 0CH 0DH 0EH 16379
             PUSH DE   0AH 0BH 0CH 0DH 0EH 16377
             POP   BC   0AH 0DH 0EH 0DH 0EH 16379
             POP   DE   0AH 0DH 0EH 0BH 0CH 16381

7.4 MESS12: DEFM 'FIRST LINE'
             DEFB 0DH   ; CR code
             DEFB 0AH   ; LF code
             DEFM 'SECOND LINE'

8.4   10010101   (-107)
           + 10010101   (-107)
             ----
       [1]   00101010   (+42)

9.4 48H - the code for the character H.

11.4 MUL4:   MACRO
             SLA
             SLA
             ENDM

12.4 (i)   D8H
     (ii) 2BH

13.4 Replace the ADC opcode by a SBC opcode.

120

```
14.4          LD    HL,HERE
              LD    DE,THERE
              LD    BC,1000
     NEXBYT:  LDI
              LD    A,(HL)
              CP    0
              JP    NZ,NEXBYT

15.4          10000010    BCD 82
            - 01010110    BCD 56
              --------
              00101100
                - 0110
              --------
              00100110    BCD 26
              --------

A.4           C7BAH                 01101101B
            - 9FF8H               + 01011110B
              ----                 --------
              27C2H                 11001011B
              ----                 --------
```

ANSWERS TO EXERCISES NUMBERED 5

1.5   10000001B

2.5   i)   35H
      ii)   79

7.5   LD   HL,TEXT
      NEXCH: LD   A,(HL)
            CP   0
            JP   Z,LASTCH
            CALL COUT
            INC   HL
            JP   NEXCH
      LASTCH: HALT
      ;
      TEXT: DEFM 'ABCDEFGHIJK'
            DEFB 0

11.5 DORP: DEFL n   ; n is 1 for display output
            -                 ; n is 0 for printer output
            -
            COND DORP
      OUTLIN: -   ; display output subroutine
            -
            RET
            ENDC
            -
            COND .NOT. DORP
      OUTLIN: -   ; printer output subroutine
            -
            RET
            ENDC
            -

12.5   Parity

            AND   OFEH   1
            SLA   A   0
            RLA   0

14.5   LD   HL,START+499
            LD   DE,START+599
            LD   BC,500
            LDDR

15.5   A
                                        -
            LD   A,43H   43H
            LD   B,28H   43H
            ADD   A,B   6BH
            DAA   71H

A.5   62EH

ANSWERS TO EXERCISES NUMBERED 6

```
1.6          INC  B

12.6 CHKPAR: BIT  0,B
             JP   Z,EVTEST
             AND  0FFH
             JP   PO,OK
             JP   NOTOK
     EVTEST: AND  0FFH
             JP   PE,OK
     NOTOK:  LD   C,1
             JP   RETSUB
     OK:     LD   C,0
     RETSUB: RET
```

14.6 6, or 0 if the block does not contain a zero value.

A.6 FBH is equivalent to 251
     A3B2H is equivalent to 41906
     142 is equivalent to 8EH
     9467 is equivalent to 24FBH

ANSWERS TO EXERCISES NUMBERED 7, 8 AND 9

14.7 Replace the instructions CPIR to HALT by

```
NEXBYT: CPI
        JP   PO,FINI    ; end of block?
        JR   NZ,NEXBYT
        LD   A,C        ; output counter
        ADD  A,30H
        CALL COUT
        LD   A,0        ; restore A
        JR   NEXBYT
;
FINI:   HALT
```

A.7 9AB3H is equivalent to 1001101010110011B
     110011101111B is equivalent to CEFH

A.8 1290 is equivalent to 50AH and 10100001010B
     101110111101B is equivalent to BBDH and 3005

A.9 Unsigned numbers in the range 0 to 1111111111111111B (FFFFH
     and 64535) can be represented in two bytes.

A.10   −1 is equivalent to 11111111B
       −2 is equivalent to 11111110B
       −126 is equivalent to 10000010B
       10000000B is equivalent to −128
       10000001B is equivalent to −127

```
A.11         11000100      -60
         +   01000110   +  +70
             --------      ---
      [1]    00001010      +10
             --------      ---


             11101001      -23
         +   11010010   +  -46
             --------      ---
      [1]    10111011      -69
             --------      ---


             01010101      +85
         -   01100000   -  +96
             --------      ---
      [1]    11110101      -11
             --------      ---


             00000101       +5
         -   10000111     --121
             --------      ----
      [1]    01111110     +126
             --------      ----
```

Index